COMPACT *Research*

Genetic Engineering

by Tamara L. Roleff

Current Issues

ReferencePoint
Press™

San Diego, CA

Picture credits:
Maury Aaseng: 34–38, 53–57, 70–73, 88–91
AP Images: 13, 18

LIBRARY OF CONGRESS CATALOGING-IN-PUBLICATION DATA

Roleff, Tamara L., 1959–
    Genetic engineering / by Tamara L. Roleff.
        p. cm. — (Compact research series)
    Includes bibliographical references and index.
    ISBN-13: 978-1-60152-038-8 (hardback)
    ISBN-10: 1-60152-038-7 (hardback)
    1. Genetic engineering—Juvenile literature. I. Title.
    QH442.R65 2008
        174'.957--dc22

                                                                    2007037707

Contents

Foreword

As modern civilization continues to evolve, its ability to create, store, distribute, and access information expands exponentially. The explosion of information from all media continues to increase at a phenomenal rate. By 2020 some experts predict the worldwide information base will double every 73 days. While access to diverse sources of information and perspectives is paramount to any democratic society, information alone cannot help people gain knowledge and understanding. Information must be organized and presented clearly and succinctly in order to be understood. The challenge in the digital age becomes not the creation of information, but how best to sort, organize, enhance, and present information.

ReferencePoint Press developed the *Compact Research* series with this challenge of the information age in mind. More than any other subject area today, researching current events can yield vast, diverse, and unqualified information that can be intimidating and overwhelming for even the most advanced and motivated researcher. The *Compact Research* series offers a compact, relevant, intelligent, and conveniently organized collection of information covering a variety of current and controversial topics ranging from illegal immigration to marijuana.

The series focuses on three types of information: objective single-author narratives, opinion-based primary source quotations, and facts and statistics. The clearly written objective narratives provide context and reliable background information. Primary source quotes are carefully selected and cited, exposing the reader to differing points of view. And facts and statistics sections aid the reader in evaluating perspectives. Presenting these key types of information creates a richer, more balanced learning experience.

For better understanding and convenience, the series enhances information by organizing it into narrower topics and adding design features that make it easy for a reader to identify desired content. For example, in *Compact Research: Illegal Immigration*, a chapter covering the economic impact of illegal immigration has an objective narrative explaining the various ways the economy is impacted, a balanced section of numerous primary source quotes on the topic, followed by facts and full-color illustrations to encourage evaluation of contrasting perspectives.

The ancient Roman philosopher Lucius Annaeus Seneca wrote, "It is quality rather than quantity that matters." More than just a collection of content, the *Compact Research* series is simply committed to creating, finding, organizing, and presenting the most relevant and appropriate amount of information on a current topic in a user-friendly style that invites, intrigues, and fosters understanding.

Genetic Engineering at a Glance

Genetic Engineering

Genetic engineering uses technology to change the genetic makeup of cells. Cloning, gene therapy, genetic enhancement, and insect- or herbicide-resistant crops are all examples of genetic engineering. All of these methods have their detractors and supporters.

Genetic Engineering in Plants

More American farmers are growing genetically modified crops that are resistant to herbicides and insect pests. Whether these plants will be responsible for a new generation of superweeds and superinsects who can feed on them is controversial.

As of 2007 no genetically modified foods were sold directly to consumers, although livestock are often fed genetically modified grains. This is due to the lack of public acceptance and the expense of genetically modified foods.

The Humane Genome Project

The Human Genome Project was a multinational effort to map and decode the human genome. It started in 1990 and finished two years ahead of schedule in 2003.

Gene Therapy

Gene therapy treats a disease or disability by replacing or repairing a faulty gene with a normal gene. Gene therapy is still in the experimental stage. While there have been a few cases of patients who have improved while undergoing gene therapy, there have also been cases of patients who died or became very ill during gene therapy trials.

Embryonic Stem Cells

Embryonic stem cells are undifferentiated cells that are collected from an embryo that is usually a few days old. If allowed to develop, embryonic stem cells can become any type of tissue or organ in the body. Some people object to the use of embryonic stem cell therapy because the collection process destroys the embryo, which they believe is a human life.

After collection, an embryonic stem cell is grown in a culture, where it grows and divides indefinitely. The resulting population of stem cells, called a line, all share the genetic characteristics of the original cell.

Federal regulations restrict all research using embryonic stem cells to embryos that were created prior to August 9, 2001, at which time there were between 60 and 70 stem cell lines available. As of 2007 there were 21 lines of embryonic stem cells available for research. Some researchers claim that the remaining stem cells are contaminated and are not good specimens for research.

Adult Stem Cells

Adult stem cells are collected after birth and are differentiated cells. They are found in bone marrow, skin, the umbilical cord, the brain, and a few other tissues. Adult stem cells generally cannot become any other type of cell other than the type of tissue where they originated; however, some research suggests that adult stem cells may be able to differentiate themselves more than originally believed.

Stem Cells and Genetic Engineering

Many scientists believe that stem cell research may eventually treat or cure diseases such as Parkinson's and Alzheimer's, spinal cord injuries, and diabetes, among others. Stem cells offer a renewable source of cells to repair or replace the damaged tissue, thus curing or treating the disease.

In order for stem cells to become an effective treatment for disease, researchers must be able to control the growth of stem cells, generate enough cells for the intended therapy, and direct the cells to differentiate into the desired tissue. In addition, the stem cells must survive and function properly in the patient after the injection, and the stem cells must not harm the patient in any way.

Human Cloning

The United States has not banned human cloning, but it has placed restrictions on human cloning research. Several states have passed their own laws regulating human cloning; some allow it for research purposes while others do not.

Because so few healthy animal clones are born, most researchers agree it is unethical to produce a human clone and implant it in a woman's womb in order to bring it to term. However, a few reproductive specialists have claimed that they have successfully cloned human babies, although none has been presented for verification.

Regulation of Genetic Engineering

The Food and Drug Administration (FDA) and the Environmental Protection Agency (EPA) regulate genetic engineering in crops and food. The FDA also regulates all research in gene therapy, and the National Institutes of Health (NIH) issues guidelines that researchers must follow when performing research in gene therapy.

Overview

"Many good things in life are filled with risks, and free people—even if properly informed about the magnitude of those risks—may choose to run them if they care enough about what they might gain thereby."

—President's Council on Bioethics, *Beyond Therapy: Biotechnology and the Pursuit of Happiness*, 2003.

"In addition to posing risks of harm that we can envision and attempt to assess, genetic engineering may also pose risks that we simply do not know enough to identify."

—Union of Concerned Scientists, "Food and Environment," 2007.

The development of genetic engineering has allowed scientists to change an organism's looks or function by adding, deleting, or re-arranging genes. The resulting technology has opened up a whole new world of possibilities in biotechnology. In agriculture, scientists have developed crops that are resistant to herbicides, insects, and rotting. They have also been able to add nutritional supplements to plants. In health, scientists are trying to cure diseases by repairing or replacing a patient's defective genes. Additionally, animals that have had genes added to their DNA are manufacturing hormones, enzymes, proteins, and even medicines. Genetic testing allows parents to test their embryos to ensure they do not have specific genetic diseases or to see if the embryo is a genetic match to be a tissue donor for a sibling. And finally, genetic engineering has been used in cloning, in which an identical copy is made from a single cell. The resulting cloned cells are sometimes used in gene therapy and other procedures.

What Is Genetic Engineering?

Genetic engineering began during the early 1970s when scientists learned recombinant DNA technology—how to cut DNA from one organism and insert it into or recombine it with another organism's DNA. They discovered an enzyme that could cut DNA strands, and scientists began to manipulate the cut strands. Researchers have developed countless ways to use genetic engineering, including transgenesis (inserting genes from one species into another), gene therapy, genetic screening, stem cell research, cloning, and therapeutic cloning.

The Genetic Engineering Controversy

Supporters of genetic engineering praise the technology because they believe it will benefit society in many ways. Genetic engineering, they claim, can help the environment, alleviate hunger around the world, provide needed medicines, treat people afflicted by serious diseases (perhaps even cure them), and potentially allow parents to choose their children's genes. Defending the use of genetic engineering to create "designer babies," Chris Seck of the *Stanford Review* writes: "The critics are right that a world with genetic engineering will contain inequalities. On the other hand, it is arguable that a world without genetic engineering, like this one, is even more unequal." Genetic engineering, he argues, levels the playing field and allows people to "fulfill their dreams and pursue their own happiness."[1]

> " Scientists have developed crops that are resistant to herbicides, insects, and rotting. They have also been able to add nutritional supplements to plants. "

However, not everyone is enthusiastic about genetic engineering. Despite its potential promise, many people are alarmed at the potential harms it could present. They are concerned about permanently changing the genetic makeup of all kinds of living organisms, from plants to livestock and other animals to people. Once an animal or species has been changed genetically, opponents point out, it can never revert back to its original genetic makeup. Still others fear that the practice of genetic enhancement will lead to eugenics, in which genetics are used to improve the human race by eliminating disabilities and undesirable characteristics. Others fear that once genetic engineering techniques are developed and refined, they will be misused. In addition, opponents note, the long-term effects and implications of genetic engineering cannot be known without follow-up studies, which have not been performed yet.

> **Despite the potential promise of genetic engineering, many people are alarmed at the potential harms it could present.**

Genetic Engineering and Agriculture

Many farmers have welcomed genetically engineered crops. Most soybeans planted have been genetically engineered to resist the herbicide glyphosate, known as Roundup. Farmers can now spray their fields with Roundup and not worry about the herbicide killing their crops. In addition, corn and cotton have been genetically engineered with a naturally occurring soil bacterium to resist insect pests that are most damaging to them. This means that farmers do not have to spray their fields as often with insecticides to kill the corn borers and boll weevils. Genetically engineered crops have higher yields, since less is lost to weeds and insect damage. Supporters of genetically engineered crops also claim that planting such crops helps the environment, since farmers spray fewer chemicals and run their tractors less, thus reducing greenhouse gases and pollutants in the air and soil.

Critics of genetically engineered crops and food maintain that changing the genetic makeup of plants and animals may make them unsafe to eat. The most common genes introduced into crops include herbicide and insect resistance, along with antibiotic resistant genes that indicate that the plant has been successfully modified. It is possible, opponents argue, that these new genes could introduce an allergen into the food where none existed before. Miguel A. Altieri, author of *Genetic Engi-*

neering in Agriculture, asserts: "No long-term studies prove the safety of [genetically modified] crops. These products are not being thoroughly tested before they arrive on the grocery shelves. Rather, they are being tested on consumers."[2]

Transgenesis

Transgenesis is the process by which genes from one species are artificially introduced into the genes of an organism of another species. For example, cotton and corn plants have been genetically modified with a bacterium that is toxic to harmful insect pests. Some tomatoes have been genetically modified with an "anti-freeze" gene from a fish to prevent the tomato from freezing in cold temperatures. Zebra fish have had a green fluorescent gene from a jellyfish added to make them glow and be more attractive to tropical fish buyers. Farm-raised salmon and trout have been modified with a gene from other fish species that make them grow up to five times faster than their wild counterparts. Finally, insulin genes from pigs have been inserted into bacteria to produce insulin for human diabetics.

> More drugs are manufactured with genetic engineering by combining genes from one organism with another.

In order for the DNA changes to be permanently passed on to the organism's progeny, the foreign DNA must be inserted into the host's germ line (egg or sperm cells). This ensures that the altered DNA is reproduced in every cell of the organism. The fastest and most efficient method of transferring genes from one species to another is through nuclear transfer, in which the nucleus with the desired DNA is transferred into an egg cell that has had its nucleus removed. Transgenesis can also be performed through modification of the organism's embryonic stem cells, but so far, this technique has only worked in mice.

Genetic Engineering and Medicine

More drugs are manufactured with genetic engineering by combining genes from one organism with another. Researchers have derived medicines from microbes (penicillin), plants (Taxol, an anticancer drug), and

Corn and cotton have been genetically engineered with a naturally occurring soil bacterium to resist insect pests that are most damaging to them. This means that farmers do not have to spray their fields as often with insecticides to kill the corn borers and boll weevils. Critics maintain that changing the genetic makeup of plants and animals may make them unsafe to eat.

animals (insulin from the pancreases of cows and pigs). Genetic engineering has made producing these drugs much faster, easier, and cheaper. Many of these drugs are produced via transgenesis. One of the first successful uses of transgenesis was interferon, a drug that stimulates the body's immune system. In 1980 researchers inserted the interferon protein into bacteria, which produced an ample supply of the protein when the bacteria multiplied. Thus scientists were able to produce the rare and expensive protein easily and cheaply. Another example of a rare and hard-to-produce protein becoming cheap and easy to obtain is insulin. Insulin for diabetics was once collected from the pancreases of cows and pigs and then purified for human use. Finally, in 1982 scientists discovered they could mass-produce human insulin by inserting the insulin gene into bacteria and replicating the bacteria.

> " Gene therapy is one of the great medical hopes of genetic engineering. "

Transgenic animals are also used as scientific research models. One of the first animals to be genetically engineered was the OncoMouse. The laboratory mice had been genetically modified to carry the oncogene, which makes the carrier especially susceptible to breast cancer. Researchers use the mice to study the progress, stages, and symptoms of the disease as well as the efficacy of treatments.

Gene Therapy

Gene therapy is one of the great medical hopes of genetic engineering. The goal of gene therapy is to repair or replace faulty or missing genes with healthy genes, thus curing the patient's disease. In order to transfer a healthy gene to a patient, researchers use a vector (usually a disabled virus that has had its viral genes removed so that it does not harm the host) of some sort. The new healthy genes are inserted into the virus and the virus is injected into the host, normally at the site or in the tissue where the researchers want the new genes to start working. The virus starts replicating itself in the host, but instead of releasing its own viral DNA, the virus "infects" the host with the healthy replacement DNA.

Gene therapy has had some success in limited trials. Ashanti DeSilva, a four-year-old girl with severe combined immunodeficiency (a severely compromised immune system that forced her to live in a sterile environment at home), was treated with gene therapy. Her doctors added a missing gene to her white blood cells and then returned the genetically modified cells to her bloodstream. The gene therapy boosted her immune system enough so that she could go to school. Researchers are hoping to learn enough about gene therapy so that it will cure diseases such as Parkinson's, Huntington's, and sickle-cell anemia.

Gene therapy does face some problems and challenges. For one, the results of the treatment are usually short-lived. The body's cells divide rapidly, thus diluting the introduced genes, which means gene therapy must be repeated often. Ashanti DeSilva had to have new gene therapy treatments every few months. Also, the body's immune system may perceive the inserted DNA as a foreign substance and reject it. There is also the possibility that the viral vector used to carry the gene into the body may recover its ability to cause disease in the patient. And finally, gene therapy is not effective for diseases or disorders that have multi-gene causes. Some patients have died while participating in gene therapy trials. Osagie K. Obasogie, who directs the project on bioethics, law, and society at the Center for Genetics and Society in Oakland, California, believes that gene therapy programs are still too risky to test on humans. "Why is an unproven procedure linked to multiple deaths being tested on people with non-fatal illnesses?"[3] he asks.

> " Scientists are researching the possibility of using stem cells to cure several diseases, such as Parkinson's, Alzheimer's, leukemia, lymphoma, diabetes, and some types of cancer. "

W. French Anderson is the former director of the Gene Therapy Laboratories at the University of Southern California's Keck School of Medicine. He performed the gene therapy on Ashanti DeSilva and believes that the promise of gene therapy outweighs the risks. Scientists, he asserts, must continue to pursue the promise offered by gene therapy. While he acknowledges that gene therapy has had its failures, he maintains that in other areas of medicine, such as transplants, successful treatments have taken years. "Gene therapy will succeed with time," he argues. "And it is important that it does succeed, because no other area of medicine holds as much promise for providing cures for the many devastating diseases that now ravage humankind."[4]

Genetic Screening and Genetic Enhancement

Genetic screening is a way to test embryos, fetuses, and adults for genetic diseases. Some parents who know that they carry a gene for a particular disease can choose to have in vitro fertilization so that the embryo can be tested for disease. Before the embryo is implanted in the woman's womb, a single cell is removed from it and tested for genetic abnormalities. Genetic screening can also be used on a fetus. Adults can be tested for genetic diseases, but genetic screening is never recommended for children under 18 years old; children generally are not mature enough to make the decision to discover if they will inherit debilitating and fatal diseases or to deal with results if the test is positive.

> "The debate over stem cell research revolves around the issue of whether embryonic stem cells should be used."

Since scientists have decoded the human genome, many human genes for physical characteristics have been identified. Some people fear that genetic enhancement—where scientists add specific genes to create an embryo based on parental requests for certain genetic traits—may be the next step. Some bioethicists and geneticists assert that parents have an obligation to want the best for their children, and that includes choosing specific characteristics for them. James D. Watson, who along with Francis Crick discovered the structure of DNA, said he "strongly favors controlling our children's genetic destinies." People should leap at the opportunity to use genetic enhancement, he maintains. "If we could make better human beings by knowing how to add genes, why shouldn't we do it?"[5] Others argue that genetic enhancement could change how parents view their children. Marcy Darnovsky, associate executive director of the Center for Genetics and Society, explains: "However subtly, the prospect—or the illusion—of selecting certain traits could make parents less likely to understand their children as emerging autonomous beings who develop in continuous interaction with their physical and social environments."[6]

Stem Cell Research

Stem cells are relatively undifferentiated cells that can transform themselves into other cells. Embryonic stem cells are pluripotent, meaning they can develop into any type of cell—blood, bone, brain, tissue, organs, and so on. Adult stem cells are multipotent, meaning they are limited in the types of cells they can become. Scientists are researching the possibility of using stem cells to cure several diseases, such as Parkinson's, Alzheimer's, leukemia, lymphoma, diabetes, and some types of cancer. A trial study of 15 patients with type 1 diabetes who were injected with stem cells drawn from their own blood found that 13 of them no longer needed daily injections of insulin, even three years after they received the stem cells.

The debate over stem cell research revolves around the issue of whether embryonic stem cells should be used. Harvesting embryonic stem cells for use in research kills the embryo. Ron Reagan, son of former president Ronald Reagan, is an advocate for embryonic stem cell research. He thinks that the research is valuable and the death of the embryo is insignificant by comparison. The promise of embryonic stem cell research, especially in the treatment of Alzheimer's disease, which afflicted his father, is important. He says embryonic stem cells are "magic" that "could revolutionize medicine."[7]

Others argue that taking the potential human life of an embryo is immoral and unjustifiable under any circumstances. This group maintains that stem cell research should use only adult stem cells, which can be taken from both children and adults. These cells are harvested from umbilical cord blood and the placenta, bone marrow, liver, skin, and the brain. The most promising research results, they assert, have come from trial studies that have used adult stem cells, not embryonic

> " Most people are concerned about the idea of intentionally cloning a human being that is a genetic identical twin to a parent or an older sibling. "

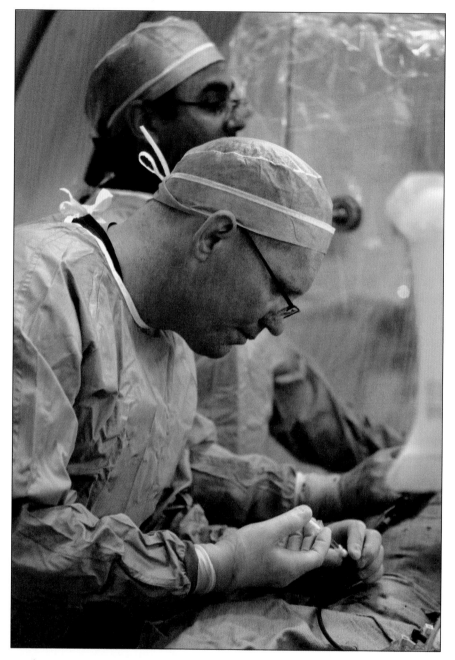

Embryonic stem cells are undifferentiated cells that are collected from an embryo that is usually a few days old. If allowed to develop, embryonic stem cells can become any type of tissue or organ in the body. Some people object to the use of embryonic stem cell therapy because the collection process destroys the embryo, which they believe is a human life.

stem cells. "Neither human embryonic-stem-cell research, . . . nor human cloning, has treated anyone of any disease,"[8] notes David Christensen of the Family Research Council.

Cloning and Therapeutic Cloning

Cloning is closely tied to stem cell research, since some scientists would like to clone embryos to use in embryonic stem cell research. In addition, some types of cloning use an enucleated (with the nucleus removed) egg cell into which a somatic (body) cell has been inserted. A chemical or electrical stimulus is used to start cell division, and if the process is successful it results in a clone of the donor cell. Dolly the sheep was created using this process, known as somatic cell nuclear transfer.

Scientists and doctors are excited about using cloning techniques to overcome the rejection issues that occur with transplant surgeries. If the healthy organ was created from tissue from the patient, then there should be no fear of the body rejecting the organ, since the tissues are genetically identical. However, many challenges and issues must be resolved before cloning can be a regular part of medical practice. First of all, cloning techniques will have to be improved, as cloning is notoriously difficult to achieve. The researchers who cloned Dolly failed 276 times before they were successful.

Reproductive cloning is a form of artificial reproduction in which an embryo is created that is an identical twin to the donor, with the intention of having a woman give birth to the clone. Most people are concerned about the idea of intentionally cloning a human being that is a genetic identical twin to a parent or an older sibling. A few people fear that people who clone themselves are extremely egotistical and are attempting to live forever through their clones. Many fear that the expectations placed on cloned humans to be exact copies of their donors would prevent the clones from being seen as individuals, completely separate and different people from their donors. Bill McKibben, author of *Enough: Staying Human in an Engineered Age*, writes that human clones would not be able to determine their own future "because in some sense their life has already been lived. . . . They would never have the sense of being their own person."[9] Those who support the use of biotechnology remind the opponents that the environment plays just as important a role in determining personality as genes; because the clone would grow up with different experiences than the donor, the clone would be a different person. Arlene Judith Klotzko, author of *A Clone of Your Own?* writes: "Would being a clone give us someone else's story to tell or retell? . . . No. . . . We are, to use another cliché, far more than the sum of our genes."[10]

Regulation

While perhaps most people would agree that genetic engineering holds great promise in all aspects, many believe that the technology must be used carefully, slowly, and with a great deal of thought as to all the possible consequences. The FDA and the EPA oversee all field trials involving genetically engineered food and crops. The U.S. Patent and Trademark Office is responsible for approving or denying patents that researchers submit for genetically engineered organisms and techniques. The FDA as well as the NIH also regulate gene therapy research trials. No federal law governs the legality of human cloning or stem cell research, although President George W. Bush placed a moratorium on all stem cell lines in the United States in August 2001. Scientists who received any kind of federal funding for their work could only use stem cell lines that were developed prior to the announcement of the moratorium.

Several countries, including Canada, Great Britain, China, and Japan, have laws regulating embryonic stem cell research. However, several states have stepped forward and enacted their own laws. While no state permits human cloning for reproduction, some states do permit embryonic cloning for research purposes while others do not. Congress has attempted on more than one occasion to ban human cloning and stem cell research, but as of 2007, no bill had become law. Bernard Siegel, president of the Genetics Policy Institute, says that if therapeutic cloning is banned, scientists will lose "the opportunity to advance the potentially greatest medical advance of our time, one that promises understanding of mankind's worst afflictions and the regeneration of tissue without rejection."[11]

The issues raised with genetic engineering will become more controversial with each new development. The main issues of contention seem to be whether a particular procedure should be done just because scientists know how to do it, and which—if any—regulations should be placed on the genetic engineering techniques.

Is Genetic Engineering Safe in Food and Agriculture?

> ❝[Genetically modified] technology will not destroy the earth, but may well make the world a safer, cleaner, and greener place in which to live.❞
>
> —C. Neal Stewart Jr., *Genetically Modified Planet: Environmental Impacts of Genetically Engineered Plants.* 2004.

> ❝There is no reason to believe that resistance to transgenic crops will not evolve among insects, weeds, and pathogens.❞
>
> —Miguel A. Altieri, *Genetic Engineering in Agriculture: The Myths, Environmental Risks, and Alternatives.* 2004.

Almost 30 years after Francis Crick and James D. Watson discovered the helix structure of genes, researchers were successful in genetically modifying a plant for the first time. The scientists, who worked for Monsanto, a multinational agricultural corporation and the manufacturer of the herbicide glyphosate known as Roundup, inserted a gene that was resistant to the antibiotic kanamycin into petunias. Normally, petunias die when exposed to kanamycin, but the genetically modified petunias prospered. Further experiments showed that the antibiotic-resistant gene existed in every cell of the plants and was passed on to future generations. Until these experiments, no one knew if genes could be inserted into new plant cells, if the modified plant cell would grow into a whole plant, if the gene would express itself in the new cell, or if the gene would be passed on to future generations of plants.

Herbicide-Resistant Crops

Now that the scientists proved the plants could be genetically modified, they started working on genetically engineering plants that would be beneficial to agriculture and society. Researchers developed genetically modified crops that were resistant to the herbicide glyphosate. These crops were called Roundup Ready after the brand name of the herbicide Roundup manufactured by Monsanto. Farmers who planted Roundup Ready crops would now be able to spray their fields with Roundup to kill weeds without fear of damaging their growing crops. Some of the Roundup Ready seeds developed were tomato, canola, cotton, corn, alfalfa, sorghum, and soybean.

Many farmers were pleased with the new herbicide-resistant crops. Roundup Ready crops were a lot less work for farmers and increased their profits. Since farmers could use Roundup, a much more effective weed killer, without fear of killing their crops, they were able to cut costs. And because it was no longer necessary to till the fields regularly to uproot new weeds, the risk of soil erosion was significantly reduced. Monsanto market manager Kurt Rahe explained how planting Roundup Ready soybeans that did not require tilling to eradicate weeds would save farmers time and money. "On a 1,000-acre farm, no-till can save as much as 450 hours of time and 3,500 gallons of diesel fuel each year. That's eleven 40-hour weeks in time savings"[12] and $10,500 less for diesel at $3.00 per gallon. A farmer who grows soybeans spelled out why he prefers the Roundup Ready crop: "The bottom line for me is that I can make more money because I spend less for herbicide applications. I get good yields with these beans, plus my soil stays on the farm instead of going down the [Mississippi] River."[13] Roundup Ready crops are also environmentally friendly since fewer tractor trips to spray and till fields produce fewer greenhouse gases that contribute to pollution and global warming.

> " **Roundup Ready crops were a lot less work for farmers and increased their profits.** "

Concerns About Roundup Ready Seeds

Others were not so sure about the benefits of Roundup Ready seeds, however. Roundup Ready crops were resistant only to the glyphosate (Roundup) herbicide; if other herbicides were sprayed on the fields, the crops would die. In the past, farmers used a mixture of herbicides and rotated among a variety of different weed killers. This exclusive use of glyphosate led some scientists and farmers to raise concerns about the development of a "superweed" that would be resistant to glyphosate. These concerns seemed justified when farmers began reporting that some weeds had developed a resistance to Roundup. These superweeds were already naturally resistant to glyphosate. They spread and cross-pollinated with genetically modified plants. According to Kristina Hubbard, a former research associate with the Center for Food Safety, the glyphosate-resistant weeds are causing farmers to "resort to more toxic and costly chemicals to control resistant weeds—the very chemicals biotechnology companies claimed Roundup Ready technology would wean out."[14]

Furthermore, organic farmers were worried that their organic crops might be contaminated by the genetically modified crops. Cross-pollination of organic and genetically modified crops would cause the organic crop to lose the right to be called organic. Farmers who grow genetically modified crops are required to keep a 900-foot buffer zone (274m) between their fields and nearby fields where genetically modified foods are not grown. However, the Idaho Alfalfa and Seed Clover Association reported in December 2006 that Roundup Ready alfalfa traits were found in alfalfa fields 2 miles (3.2km) from the nearest Roundup Ready fields. The transgenic material was in high enough quantities to keep the crop from being sold as organic, thus reducing its profitability, according to the association.

> " This exclusive use of glyphosate led some scientists and farmers to raise concerns about the development of a "superweed." "

In addition to developing glyphosate-resistant plants, researchers also developed plants that were resistant to insects. Corn borers, which cause broken stalks and dropped ears of corn, can reduce crop yields by 25 percent. Cotton fields are plagued by budworms and bollworms that can produce three to five generations of pests in a single growing season and reduce the crop's yield by 20 percent or more. Crops that could resist corn borers, budworms, and bollworms would greatly increase a farmer's yield and profits. Spraying fields with insecticide is expensive and time-consuming, and the insecticide can drift during spraying, harming nearby crop fields. Furthermore, insecticide kills beneficial insects as well as harmful insects, and some insect pests have developed a resistance to chemical sprays.

> " The introduction of [*Bacillus thuringiensis*] into the plant's genes . . . allows the plant to produce a toxin poisonous to pests. "

Scientists discovered that the toxic bacterium *Bacillus thuringiensis* (known by its shortened name Bt) occurs naturally and widely in soil. Different varieties of the Bt microbe will kill moths, while another one kills beetles, and yet another one kills flies. The specificity of the bacterium's genes allows scientists to use Bt as an insecticide against different insect pests. Bt proteins were introduced into the genes of selected crops such as corn, potatoes, soybeans, and cotton. The introduction of Bt into the plant's genes, and therefore into its own living tissue, allows the plant to produce a toxin poisonous to pests. After taking just a few bites of the genetically modified plant, the insect dies. Agricultural economists Graham Brookes and Peter Barfoot estimated in a 2005 paper that genetically modified "crops have contributed to a significant reduction in the global environmental impact of production agriculture."[15] Genetically modified crops have been planted since 1996, and Brooks and Barfoot estimated that in just 9 years, the amount of pesticides sprayed globally had been reduced by 6 percent, or 379 million pounds (172 million kg).

Claims That Bt Is Not Safe and Benign

Despite the claimed benefits to the environment, not everyone was so enamored of the genetically engineered crops. Jeffrey M. Smith, executive director of the Institute for Responsible Technology, argues that the gene for Bt toxin inserted into plants is not safe and benign to humans and mammals, as previously assumed. He notes that when plants are genetically engineered with Bt, the toxin "is thousands of times more concentrated than the spray version"[16] and those who are exposed to the Bt toxin are more likely to have an allergic response. According to Italian scientist Manuela Malatesta, the Bt levels in crops fed to lab mice was "as potent as cholera toxin"[17] and that the animals' immune systems were compromised and extremely sensitive to formerly harmless substances.

The Flavr Savr Tomato

In 1994 a California-based company called Calgene released a tomato on the market known as the Flavr Savr. The tomato had been genetically engineered so that it could ripen on the vine and then be shipped to market without the typical problems of bruising and rotting during shipment. To allay any fears about the tomato, Calgene asked the FDA to perform safety tests on the tomato. The FDA ruled that the anti-rotting gene introduced into the Flavr Savr tomato did not pose any risk to the consumer and was "as safe as tomatoes bred by conventional means."[18] Three years later, Canada also approved the sale of the Flavr Savr tomato. But despite being approved by the U.S. and Canadian governments, Calgene pulled the Flavr Savr tomato from the market. Consumers felt the cost of the tomato was too high and the tomato's flavor was not significantly improved over green tomatoes, and many people were fearful of eating a genetically modified food.

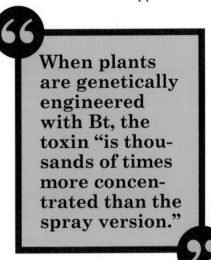

When plants are genetically engineered with Bt, the toxin "is thousands of times more concentrated than the spray version."

Golden Rice

Such fears have also plagued Golden Rice, a rice that has been genetically fortified with beta-carotene. The human body converts beta-carotene (which gives carrots their orange color and makes Golden Rice golden) into vitamin A. Developers hoped the rice could alleviate the symptoms of vitamin A deficiency in poor citizens in developing nations. Vitamin A deficiency can cause blindness in children, severe anemia, a compromised immune system, an increased risk of death from measles and other childhood diseases, and malaria. Half the world's population receives 80 percent of its calories from white rice, which does not provide beta-carotene or vitamin A. According to the United Nations Children's Fund, 124 million children suffer from vitamin A deficiency.

> **People who eat Golden Rice will experience improvements in their health problems that are caused by vitamin A deficiency.**

According to the inventors of the fortified rice, people who eat Golden Rice will experience improvements in their health problems that are caused by vitamin A deficiency. The initial Golden Rice strains contained microgram units of beta-carotene in the single digits. As of 2005 Golden Rice produces 23 times more beta-carotene per gram than the original Golden Rice; enough, the rice's developers say, that people who eat "Golden Rice on a nearly daily basis would be able to maintain an appropriate vitamin A blood level and thus also be able to have a sufficient provitamin A uptake from diet."[19] The two European plant researchers who developed Golden Rice formed a humanitarian organization, Golden Rice Project, which will work with the World Health Organization and the United Nations Food and Agricultural Organization to distribute the rice seeds free of charge in developing countries. These organizations see Golden Rice as a simple and inexpensive solution to a global dietary problem.

Concerns About Genetically Modified Foods

The biggest concern critics had about Golden Rice was the low amount of beta-carotene in the rice, which would require a person to eat between three and four pounds of rice a day. But with higher levels of beta-carotene in the rice, the recommended daily allowance of beta-carotene can be reached by eating 5 to 6 ounces (142 to 170 g) per day. With that objection out of the way, critics turned to more general objections of genetically modified food. Greenpeace, for example, opposes all genetically modified foods on principle, concerned that genetic engineering may introduce an unknown protein into the food, triggering allergic reactions—or worse—

in consumers. Due to the wide variety of genetic modifications that are performed on food crops, a food with no previous history of allergens could suddenly become allergenic to millions of people.

In addition, researchers usually insert an antibiotic-resistant gene as a "marker" gene into the plant. If the plant is no longer affected by the antibiotic (such as kanamycin in petunias), then researchers know that the plant has been successfully genetically modified. However, many people fear that these antibiotic-resistant genes could affect human health if people ate genetically modified food. If a person was being treated for an infection with kanamycin and then ate some genetically modified food in which a kanamycin-resistant gene was used as a gene marker, then the resistance gene would inactivate the antibiotic, and the kanamycin would be ineffective in treating the infection. Miguel A. Altieri, an associate professor and associate entomologist at the University of California, Berkeley, sums up the dangers of genetically modifying the food supply:

> No scientist can negate the possibility that changing the fundamental genetic makeup of a food could cause new diseases or heath problems. No long-term studies prove the safety of [genetically modified] crops. These products are not being thoroughly tested before they arrive on the grocery store shelves. Rather, they are being tested on consumers.[20]

As researchers study the effects of genetic engineering of crops and food, both the benefits and risks of genetic engineering are being challenged. This chapter investigates some of the issues that supporters and opponents argue over, including the effectiveness of Roundup Ready and Bt crops and genetically modified foods.

Is Genetic Engineering Safe in Food and Agriculture?

66 **Meat and milk from clones of adult cattle, pigs and goats, and their offspring, are as safe to eat as food from conventionally bred animals.** 99

—Food and Drug Administration, "FDA Issues Draft Documents on the Safety of Animal Clones," December 28, 2006. www.fda.gov.

The Food and Drug Administration is a federal agency charged with overseeing and protecting the nation's food supply.

66 **The Food and Drug Administration's assessment that food from cloned animals is safe to eat is a victory for biotech companies and a loss for everyone else.** 99

—*New York Times*, "Safe as Milk?" January 6, 2007.

The *New York Times* is a leading American newspaper based in New York City.

Bracketed quotes indicate conflicting positions.

* Editor's Note: While the definition of a primary source can be narrowly or broadly defined, for the purposes of Compact Research, a primary source consists of: 1) results of original research presented by an organization or researcher; 2) eyewitness accounts of events, personal experience, or work experience; 3) first-person editorials offering pundits' opinions; 4) government officials presenting political plans and/or policies; 5) representatives of organizations presenting testimony or policy.

❝Tinkering with the genes of an organism can have re-percussions far beyond the 'minor' modification intended by biotech scientists.❞

—David Suzuki, "Transgenic Canola Not Friendly to Bees, Butterflies," April 1, 2005. www.davidsuzuki.org.

Suzuki, an award-winning geneticist and environmentalist, is the founder of the David Suzuki Foundation, an environmental organization that works to conserve nature and help achieve sustainability within a generation.

❝For all the yet-to-be-proven costs and unidentified harms that could potential[ly] result from genetic modification, there also exist a number of certain, identifiable, and easily proven harms that come from not embracing new technology, too.❞

—Radley Balko, "Genetically Modified Food: An Environmental Risk, or Millions' Best Hope for Survival?" September 21, 2006. www.aworldconnected.org.

Balko, a freelance writer and former policy analyst with the Cato Institute, is a senior editor for *Reason* magazine and a columnist for *FoxNews.com*.

❝This is not a sustainable technology. It's being overused, resistant weeds are growing. So now growers, more and more instead of having to use a single herbicide when the crop was first developed, are now being recommended to [use] what's called tank mix with other herbicides that can also be dangerous.❞

—Doug Gurian-Sherman, "Are Genetically Modified Crops Safe?" *Talk of the Nation*, May 5, 2006. www.npr.org.

Gurian-Sherman is a senior scientist for the Center for Food Safety, International Center for Technology Assessment in Washington, D.C.

"With Bt cotton, . . . farmers can spray [insecticides] much less, and the poison contained in the plant is delivered only to the bugs that actually eat the crop."

—Jonathan Rauch, "Will Frankenfood Save the Planet?" *Atlantic Monthly*, October 2003.

Rauch is a senior writer for the *National Journal* magazine, a correspondent for *Atlantic Monthly*, and a guest scholar for the Brookings Institution, a Washington, D.C., think tank.

"It can even be argued that certain [genetically modified] crops that are resistant to, for example, herbicide or pests, are exposed to far less chemical contamination than most of the food we eat. So clearly it is possible that [genetically modified] food is not, in fact bad for us at all."

—Conor Meade, "Careful Stewardship of GM Crops Is Needed, Not a Ban," *Irish Times*, June 23, 2007.

Meade is the coauthor of the 2005 paper "GM Crop Cultivation in Ireland: Ecological and Economic Considerations for Proceedings of the Royal Irish Academy." www.ria.ie.

"[Genetically modified] seeds and chemicals are a threat to farmers' survival, a threat to consumer health and a threat to the environment."

—Vandana Shiva, "In Praise of Cowdung," November 12, 2002. www.zmag.org.

Shiva of New Delhi, India, is a physicist, ecofeminist, environmental activist, and the author of numerous books and articles on agriculture, food, biodiversity, and genetic engineering.

66 [Genetically modified] crops have nothing to do with solving hunger; in fact, there is a good chance [genetically modified] agriculture will lead to catastrophic famine in the world by greatly decreasing the gene pool of plants.**99**

—David Kennell, "Genetically Engineered Plant Crops: Potential for Disaster," *Synthesis/Regeneration*, Fall 2004.

Kennell is professor emeritus at the Department of Molecular Microbiology, Washington School of Medicine.

66 Our custom of eating food that has been genetically modified is actually thousands of years old.**99**

—James D. Watson with Andrew Berry, *DNA: The Secret of Life*. New York: Knopf, 2003.

Watson, along with Francis Crick, discovered the structure of the DNA molecule, and along with Maurice Wilkins, received the Nobel Prize for Physiology or Medicine in 1962. Berry is a fruit fly geneticist and a research associate at Harvard University's Museum of Comparative Zoology.

66 No environmentalist can point to a single person who's been killed or even injured by a genetically modified food.**99**

—*Investor's Business Daily*, "Let Them Eat Cake," November 28, 2006.

Investor's Business Daily is a leading business newspaper that covers the key issues in economics, politics, and culture.

"If we could get more of this golden rice, which is a genetically modified strain of rice, especially rich in vitamin A, out to the developing world, it could save 40,000 lives a day, people that are malnourished and dying."

—Bill Clinton, "Remarks Prior to Discussions with Prime Minister Tony Blair of the United Kingdom and an Exchange with Reporters in Okinawa," July 23, 2000.

Clinton was the forty-second president of the United States.

"The current [genetically modified] wonder crop, Syngenta's 'Golden Rice,' promises not only cheap and plentiful food but a cure for the millions of people suffering from vitamin A deficiency. Companies like Syngenta will tell you that the common sense solution to vitamin A deficiency, a balanced diet, is a luxury beyond the reach of the people they are trying to help, conveniently missing out the fact that these people had a balanced diet until companies like Syngenta introduced new agricultural technologies that wiped out everything in their fields except rice."

—Graham Thompson, "Debate: Genetically Modified Food and the WTO Ruling," *Ethical Corporation*, April 4, 2006.

Thompson is an activist for Greenpeace UK.

Is Genetic Engineering Safe in Food and Agriculture?

- Genes from bacteria, viruses, animals, and even humans have been inserted into plants such as soybeans, corn, canola, cotton, and rice to **genetically modify them**.

- An **"anti-freeze"** gene that allows flounder to survive in very cold water has been inserted into tomatoes to increase their tolerance to frost.

- It is estimated that **21 percent** of all corn and **17 percent** of all cotton planted in the United States in 2007 were genetically engineered with insect-resistant Bt.

- In 2007, **91 percent** of all soybeans planted were genetically engineered to resist herbicides.

- Approximately **60 percent** of Americans surveyed in 2006 were not aware that genetically modified foods are being grown, and only **25 percent** realized that genetically modified foods have been for sale in the United States for more than a decade.

- The pink bollworm causes more than **$32 million in losses** to cotton crops every year; and so far, insecticides, sterilization techniques, and genetically modified cotton have not been able to eradicate it.

Americans Support Regulation of Genetically Modified Food

Though most consumers revealed that they knew little about federal regulation of genetically modified foods, among those who claimed to have heard about biotech regulation, a majority of voters favor increased regulation of genetically modified foods.

Generally speaking, do you think there is too much, too little, or the right amount of regulation of genetically modified foods?

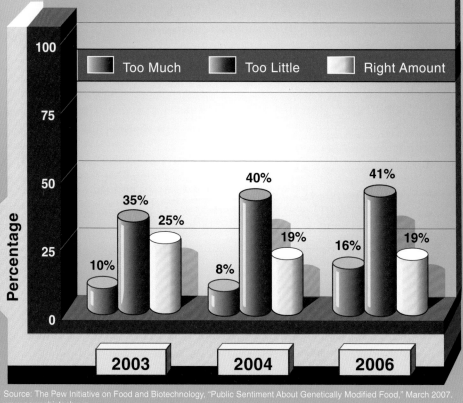

Source: The Pew Initiative on Food and Biotechnology, "Public Sentiment About Genetically Modified Food," March 2007. www.pewagbiotech.org.

- Three federal agencies **oversee genetically modified plants:** the FDA, the EPA, and the U.S. Department of Agriculture.

Global Prevalence of Vitamin A Deficiency

At the beginning of the twenty-first century, 124 million people, in 118 countries mostly in Africa and South East Asia, were estimated to be affected by Vitamin A Deficiency (VAD). Vitamin A Deficiency is responsible for 1 to 2 million deaths and 500,000 cases of irreversible blindness. Children and pregnant women are at highest risk.

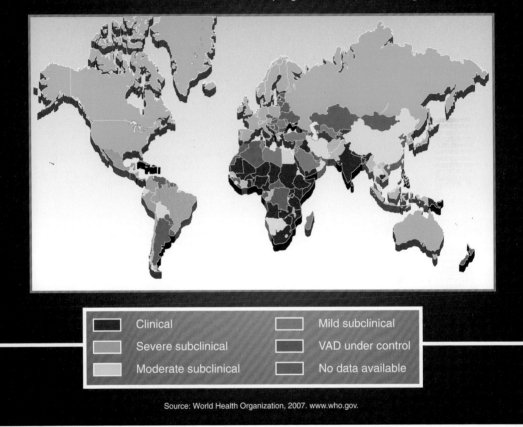

Clinical — Mild subclinical

Severe subclinical — VAD under control

Moderate subclinical — No data available

Source: World Health Organization, 2007. www.who.gov.

- More than **35 countries have restrictions** on the importation of genetically modified food.

- In order to adequately feed the world by 2050, the amount of food produced will have to **increase by 50 percent.**

- Approximately **250 million acres** (101 million ha) were planted with genetically modified plants in 2005.

Opposition to Genetically Modified Foods Has Declined

Support for genetically modified foods has remained fairly flat since 2001, when just 26 percent of Americans favored the introduction of genetically modified foods into the U.S. food supply, and 58 percent opposed. Since 2001, opposition has declined from 58 percent to 46 percent—a drop of over 20 percent—while support has been stable, at 27 percent in 2006.

Do you favor or oppose the introduction of genetically modified foods into the U.S. food supply?

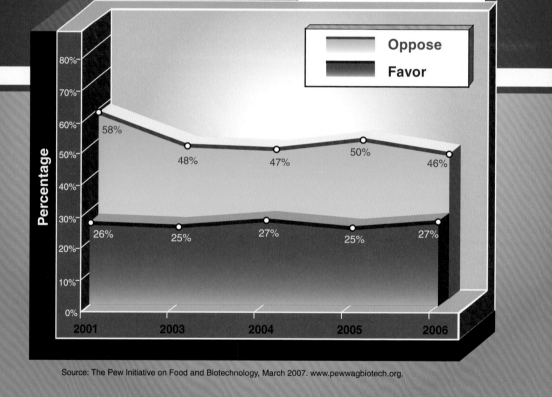

Source: The Pew Initiative on Food and Biotechnology, March 2007. www.pewwagbiotech.org.

- Food industry companies say they believe that **mandatory biotech food labeling** would be perceived by consumers as a warning rather than an informational tool.

Genetically Engineered Crops Make Up a Large Percentage of Crops Planted

The National Agricultural Statistics Service randomly selects farmers across the United States each year and asks if they planted corn, soybeans, or cotton seed that, through biotechnology, is resistant to herbicides, insects, or both. Stacked gene varieties include only those containing biotech traits for both herbicide and insect resistance.

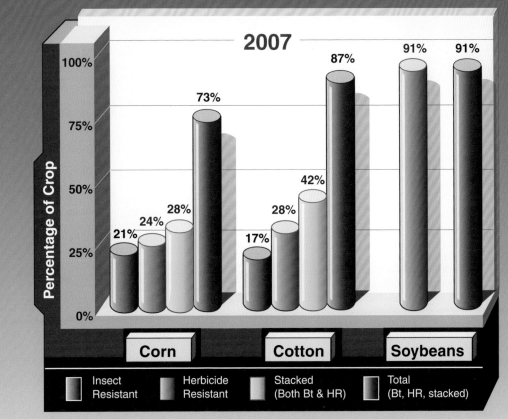

2007

	Insect Resistant	Herbicide Resistant	Stacked (Both Bt & HR)	Total (Bt, HR, stacked)
Corn	21%	24%	28%	73%
Cotton	17%	28%	42%	87%
Soybeans		91%		91%

Source: National Agricultural Statistics Service, U.S. Department of Agriculture, June 29, 2007. www.usda.gov.

- A Canadian study estimated that mandatory labeling of biotech food would cost consumers **$700 to $950 million annually.**

Golden Rice Delivers Vitamin A

In rice-based studies, Golden Rice, a rice that has been genetically fortified with beta-carotene, delivers more than the recommended daily allowance of vitamin A (after conversion from beta-carotene) to women and children. This diagram shows that even with the very low dietary intake of vitamin A from other sources, a rice that has been genetically fortified with beta-carotene could fully provide the daily needs of women and children.

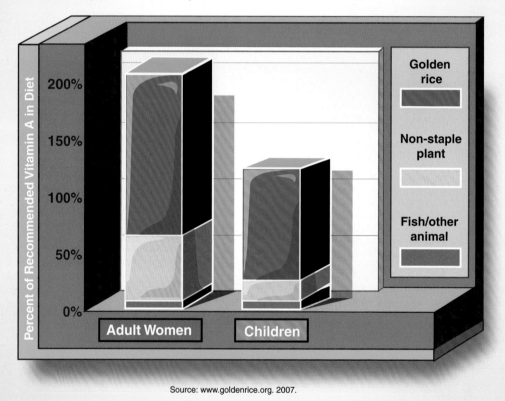

Source: www.goldenrice.org. 2007.

- A survey of consumers found **81 percent** supported mandatory labeling of genetically engineered food.

- Many countries require **mandatory labeling** of genetically modified foods.

Is Genetic Engineering Safe in Humans?

> ❝No gene therapy treatment has ever been deemed safe or effective enough to receive [Food and Drug Administration] approval.❞
>
> —Osagie K. Obasogie, "Gene Therapy Risky Business for Patients," 2007.

> ❝The first people to go through any particular gene therapy will be those who are extremely ill. . . . Given the choice between a debilitating disease one knows and a possible cure with unknown side effects, many sick and injured will choose the latter.❞
>
> —Ramez Naam, *More than Human: Embracing the Promise of Biological Enhancement*, 2005.

Human genetic engineering encompasses a wide spectrum of genetic research. It includes research already underway, including genetic screening for disease and disabilities, and gene therapy, in which a faulty gene is replaced with a normal gene. It also includes futuristic premises, such as genetic enhancement, a theory in which parents can order "designer babies" with specific traits and characteristics.

Preimplantation Genetic Diagnosis

Genetic screening is available for use both before and after birth. Prenatal testing is used on an embryo or fetus to screen for chromosomal disorders such as Down syndrome or genetic abnormalities such as Tay-Sachs disease, cystic fibrosis, or sickle-cell anemia. If these genes are present, parents can choose another embryo to implant or abort the pregnancy, if desired. Prenatal testing can also be used to determine the fetus's gender. Finally, prenatal genetic screening is occasionally used to determine if the embryo is a genetic match for a sibling who needs a tissue donor.

> Many genetic diseases and disorders can be diagnosed during pregnancy.

Many genetic diseases and disorders can be diagnosed during pregnancy, but if the result is positive, the parents-to-be then need to make the difficult decision of whether the pregnancy should be terminated. An alternative is to test an embryo before it has been implanted into the woman's uterus, but in order to use this procedure, the couple must undergo in vitro fertilization, in which eggs are taken from the woman and fertilized in a petri dish. When the embryo is two to three days old, a procedure known as preimplantation genetic diagnosis (PGD) tests the DNA from a single cell for genetic abnormalities. Doctors can examine the cell for potential birth defects or fatal diseases, such as cystic fibrosis, Huntington's disease, hemophilia, muscular dystrophy, and sickle-cell anemia. Embryos with abnormalities are discarded, while genetically healthy embryos are implanted in the woman's uterus. PGD allows parents who are carriers of a genetic disease to have children with the assurance that their child will not inherit the disease.

PGD has only been in use since 1989 and still remains a rare procedure. It is estimated that only a few thousand procedures are performed each year around the world. Anuja Dokras, a physician in the department of obstetrics and gynecology at Yale University School of Medicine, writes that PGD "is currently available to couples whose offspring are at a high risk (25–50 percent) for a specific genetic condition due to one or both parents being carriers or affected by the disease."[21]

Despite the good intentions of those who perform PGD, the procedure has come under fire by pro-life activists and others who believe it is unethical to manipulate or discard human embryos. Josephine Quintavalle, director of the group Comment on Reproductive Ethics, said,

"PGD is currently nothing more than a weapon of destruction, aimed at the ruthless elimination of any embryo which does not conform to eugenic concepts of perfection."[22]

Tissue Donors

There are several life-threatening diseases in which the only cure is a tissue transplant—such as blood or bone marrow—from a compatible donor. Many times the sick patient has no family members who are a close genetic match, in which case, some parents have been known to undergo in vitro fertilization to produce embryos that can be analyzed by PGD to determine if they are a genetic match to the ill sibling. Compatible embryos are implanted into the mother's womb to produce a sibling for the ill child. After the baby's birth, a doctor uses stem or blood cells from the umbilical cord or a sampling of the baby's bone marrow and injects it into the patient. Norman Fost, a medical ethicist at the University of Wisconsin, wrote an editorial in *Journal of the American Medical Association* asserting that the procedure saves lives. He noted that before PGD was available, parents would conceive babies naturally in the hopes that it would be a genetic match to their sick child, but there was only a one-in-four chance that it would be a match. Some women would abort the baby if prenatal tests showed it would not be a suitable donor. Tissue typing through PGD usually does not result in abortion, he notes, and does not present a risk to the embryo. "Of all the reasons people have babies, this would seem to be a wonderful reason,"[23] Fost wrote.

> "Genetic testing can be extremely helpful in determining if a person is a carrier for a genetic disorder or for diseases that are closely linked to abnormalities or mutations on specific genes."

Opponents of creating designer babies for tissue matches say the procedure is unethical. Samuel Hensley, a fellow at that Center for Bioethics and Human Dignity in Illinois, says that from a Christian perspective, each embryo created is a human life. Destroying or discarding the unused embryos is contrary to the Christian view in which human life is sacred. Another serious ethical concern, according to Hensley, is that a "human life would be created for the purpose of benefiting others. . . . Should a child be created specifically to save another person's life, or should a child be welcomed and loved unconditionally regardless of his or her instrumental value in helping someone else?"[24]

Genetic Screening

Genetic testing can be extremely helpful in determining if a person is a carrier for a genetic disorder or for diseases that are closely linked to abnormalities or mutations on specific genes. For example, women can be tested to see if they are at an increased risk for breast cancer; mutations in the genes *BRCA1* and *BRCA2* are often found in women who develop breast cancer. However, 20 percent to 40 percent of women with the *BRCA1* and *BRCA2* mutations do not develop breast cancer. And many women who do have breast cancer do not have the gene mutations. So while the test for genetic mutations may be a good indicator that a woman's chances of developing breast cancer are higher than average, it is not definitive.

The practice of testing for genetic diseases and disabilities is controversial.

The practice of testing for genetic diseases and disabilities is controversial. Some women with the breast cancer gene may decide to have a mastectomy, even if they have not yet been diagnosed with breast cancer. Presymptomatic testing for genetic disease can be very emotional and distressing, and is never recommended for children under 18. It may also make the patient worried about becoming ill, strain family relationships, especially with siblings, and could lead to problems with employers or insurance companies.

Gene Therapy

There are two types of gene therapy: somatic gene therapy, in which someone with a genetic disease, such as cystic fibrosis, is treated with healthy genes in the hopes that the healthy genes will "infect" the patient's cells and replace the faulty genes, thus lessening or curing the disease; and germ-line gene therapy, also known as genetic enhancement. The genes inserted during somatic gene therapy cannot be inherited and will not be transferred to any offspring. Germ-line gene therapy modifies genes in the sex (germ) cells, resulting in changes that can be inherited by the patient's children.

Gene therapy has been used to treat people with Parkinson's disease, a degenerative and incurable disorder of the central nervous system that affects the person's motor skills and speech. In one study of Parkinson's patients who had undergone gene therapy, researchers reported gene therapy reduced the patients' symptoms by as much as 70 percent, with a 25 percent to 30 percent improvement in the symptoms of all patients in the study group. Matthew During, the lead researcher of the experimental procedure, said of the results, "It's one of the biggest successes of gene therapy so far." One patient had spectacular results, During said. "It is now four years since the first patient was treated, and he's now riding his bike. When we first met him, he couldn't even hold a glass of water."[25] Not everyone is convinced of the therapy's effectiveness, however. Jon Stoessl, who works with Parkinson's patients at the University of British Columbia in Vancouver, said Parkinson's patients are known to suffer from the placebo effect—in which patients improve no matter what the treatment is simply because they have high expectations for their treatment.

> " Gene therapy has been used to treat people with Parkinson's disease. "

Genetic Enhancement

Breakthroughs in genetic engineering may soon allow parents to choose their children's genes in a process known as genetic enhancement. Some bioethicists contend that genetic enhancement of babies is most likely inevitable. In the future, parents who want to give their children every advantage may be able to give their children better memories, stronger muscles, and longer lives, as well as perhaps an inclination toward math or music, or a specific eye or hair color.

Some researchers believe that research into genetic enhancement should continue because it will lead to other more promising treatments. Ramez Naam, author of *More than Human*, writes:

Promising research on curing Alzheimer's disease, on reducing the incidence of heart disease and cancer, on restoring sight to the blind and motion to the paralyzed is the very same research that could lead to keeping us young, improving our memories, wiring our minds together, or enhancing ourselves in other ways. We cannot stop research into enhancing ourselves without also halting research focused on healing the sick and injured.[26]

> **Parkinson's patients are known to suffer from the placebo effect—in which patients improve no matter what the treatment is simply because they have high expectations for their treatment.**

Julian Savulescu, the Uehiro Professor of Practical Ethics at Oxford University, contends that parents should enhance their children's health and well-being in any way they can, and that includes genetic enhancement. According to Savulescu, if genetic enhancement "can provide us with the ability to enhance more effectively our children's well-being, to give them better opportunities of a better life, to fail to do so will be to be responsible for the consequences, including their unhappiness."[27]

Designer Babies

Detractors of genetic enhancement call the potential children of such procedures "designer babies" because in theory, at least, the parents could "order" the genes they would like the child to have: its gender, hair and eye color, body type or athleticism, intelligence, musical inclinations, and so forth. Mark Frankel, the director of the Scientific Freedom, Responsibility and Law Program in the American Association for the Advancement of Science, says genetically engineered babies could fundamentally alter the relationship between parents and children, and impose some sort of conditionality on the love that a parent might feel for the child.

When a couple becomes pregnant they know they are

expecting a child, they don't know they are expecting a particular child, whereas in the future they may be able to design an embryo in such a way that once it's implanted and grows they will have specific expectations about that child. That he or she will be stronger, more athletic, intelligent, whatever the case may be. If there's a failure along the way and this doesn't happen one has to raise the issue of how that parent will view that child given that it now might not live up to expectations.[28]

According to Frankel, if parents expect their genetically enhanced child to have blond hair and blue eyes and be musically gifted, and instead their child has brown hair and brown eyes and has no musical abilities, the parents are bound to be disappointed that their child does not meet their expectations. And the disappointment may transfer over to how they interact with and love the child.

Eugenics

Naam, Savulescu, and other supporters of genetic enhancement are emphatic that genetic enhancement is not eugenics. They assert that eugenics is a state-sponsored program designed to weed out the physically and mentally disabled by ridding the gene pool of "bad" genes, which they call "negative eugenics." When individuals strive to increase the frequency of "good" genes in their children, geneticists call it "positive eugenics." Savulescu explains: "We practice eugenics when we screen for Down's syndrome, and other chromosomal or genetic abnormalities. The reason we don't define that sort of thing as 'eugenics,' as the Nazis did, is because it's based on choice. It's about enhancing people's freedom rather than reducing it."[29]

> " Breakthroughs in genetic engineering may soon allow parents to choose their children's genes in a process known as genetic enhancement. "

Despite these arguments opponents of genetic enhancement declare that the procedure is indeed eugenics, with all the negative connotations the word implies. They also voice ethical concerns about the procedure. Marilyn E. Coors, an assistant professor of bioethics and genetics at the University of Colorado and the secretariat for the U.S. Conference of Catholic Bishops, writes, "Genetic enhancement has emerged as an ethical issue because it involves the power to redesign ourselves, including the potential to impact the very essence of what it means to be human."[30]

The issues raised by genetic engineering of humans are destined to become more controversial as knowledge of biotechnology continues to expand. The fundamental issue is whether humans are attempting to play God when they alter human genes. Although in the present, human genetic engineering remains in the theory stage, researchers, doctors, ethicists, and the general population should be prepared for the day when "someday" becomes "today."

Is Genetic Engineering Safe in Humans?

66 **We are manipulating the very basic instructions that govern life on Earth, yet our knowledge of how genes are incorporated into hierarchies of organization and function remains spotty and incomplete.** 99

—David Suzuki, "A Little Knowledge," *New Scientist*, September 23, 2006.

Suzuki, an award-winning geneticist, is the cofounder of the David Suzuki Foundation, a Canadian organization that combines science and education to protect the environment and human health.

66 **Gene therapy will succeed with time. And it is important that it does succeed, because no other area of medicine holds as much promise for providing cures for the many devastating diseases that now ravage humankind.** 99

—W. French Anderson, "The Best of Times, the Worst of Times," *Science*, April 28, 2000.

Anderson is the former director of gene therapy at the University of Southern California Medical School. He was the first person to attempt authorized somatic gene transfer experiments on humans by inserting healthy genes into Ashanti DeSilva, a four-year-old girl with severe combined immunodeficiency.

Bracketed quotes indicate conflicting positions.

* Editor's Note: While the definition of a primary source can be narrowly or broadly defined, for the purposes of Compact Research, a primary source consists of: 1) results of original research presented by an organization or researcher; 2) eyewitness accounts of events, personal experience, or work experience; 3) first-person editorials offering pundits' opinions; 4) government officials presenting political plans and/or policies; 5) representatives of organizations presenting testimony or policy.

66 In just a few decades, we've gone from the first tinkering with human genes to the discovery of dozens of techniques that could alter the human genome in very precise ways. 99

—Ramez Naam, *More than Human: Embracing the Promise of Biological Enhancement.* New York: Broadway, 2005.

Naam is the author of *More than Human: Embracing the Promise of Biological Enhancement.*

66 The moral quandary arises when people use [gene] therapy not to cure a disease but to reach beyond health, to enhance their physical or cognitive capacities, to lift themselves above the norm. 99

—Michael J. Sandel, "The Case Against Perfection," *Atlantic Monthly*, April 2004.

Sandel, a professor of government at Harvard University, is a member of the President's Council on Bioethics.

66 The first phase of regenerative science will be to use our own genes, proteins and antibodies as medicines to rebuild our bodies from the inside out. All we are doing, really, is stimulating the body's inherent regenerative capacity. 99

—William Haseltine, "Regenerative Medicine: Where the Genetic and Info Revolutions Converge," *New Perspectives Quarterly*, Fall 2004.

Haseltine is chair and chief executive officer of Human Genome Sciences, a gene-based pharmaceutical product manufacturer.

❝Keeping in mind that most traits of interest to parents seeking better children are heavily influenced by environment, even successful genetic screening and embryo selection might not, in many cases, produce the desired result.❞

—President's Council on Bioethics, *Beyond Therapy: Biotechnology and the Pursuit of Happiness*. Washington, DC: Government Printing Office, 2003.

The President's Council on Bioethics advises the president of the United States on bioethical issues.

❝Far from being unnatural, the drive to alter and improve on ourselves is a fundamental part of who we humans are.❞

—Ramez Naam, *More than Human: Embracing the Promise of Biological Enhancement*. New York: Broadway, 2005.

Naam is the author of *More than Human: Embracing the Promise of Biological Enhancement*.

❝Creating life primarily to serve someone else, especially when the other life may be rejected and destroyed for the simple reason that it did not meet the parents' needs, is an action that should always be condemned.❞

—Samuel Hensley, "Designer Babies: One Step Closer," Center for Bioethics and Human Dignity, July 1, 2004. www.cbhd.org.

Hensley, a fellow at the Center for Bioethics and Human Dignity, is a surgical pathologist at Mississippi Baptist Medical Center in Jackson, Mississippi, and an assistant clinical professor at the University of Mississippi School of Medicine.

❝It is hard to see why an unborn child has any obligation to preserve the genetic diversity of the species at the price of grave harm or certain death.❞

—Arthur L. Caplan, "If Gene Therapy Is the Cure, What Is the Disease?" *Bioethics.net*, November 8, 2002. www.bioethics.net.

Caplan is the director of the Center for Bioethics at the University of Pennsylvania School of Medicine and the chair of the department of medical ethics.

❝The possibilities for germline engineering go beyond the elimination of disease and open the door for modifications to human longevity, increased intelligence, increased muscle mass, and many other types of genetic enhancements. . . . It opens the door to the alteration of the human species.❞

—Stephen L. Baird, "Designer Babies: Eugenics Repackaged or Consumer Options?" *Technology Teacher*, April 2007.

Baird is a technology education teacher at Bayside Middle School, Virginia Beach, Virginia, and adjunct faculty member at Old Dominion University.

❝There is no overriding objection to using technological means to modify our own personalities, and ultimately to reshape human nature.❞

—Russell Blackford, "It's OK to Change Your Mind," Institute for Ethics and Emerging Technologies, July 22, 2004. http://ieet.org.

Blackford is a fellow at the Institute for Ethics and Emerging Technologies.

66 If [genetic technology] can provide us with the ability to enhance more effectively our children's well-being, to give them better opportunities of a better life, to fail to do so will be to be responsible for the consequences, including their unhappiness. 99

—Julian Savulescu, quoted in Australian Society for Medical Research, "Expert Says Genetic Technology Could Enhance Our Children's Well-Being," June 8, 2005. www.asmr.org.

Savulescu is the Uehiro Professor of Practical Ethics at Oxford University, England, where he specializes in the ethics of genetics and the ethics of embryo research.

66 Fiddling with the heritable DNA of humans to make them smarter, faster, or more pious—or more deaf . . . is playing God not just with a particular embryo but with our species. 99

—Nicholas D. Kristof, "Birth Without the Bother?" *New York Times*, July 23, 2007.

Kristof is a syndicated columnist for the *New York Times*.

66 The potential of [gene therapy] to lift the curse of genetic disease is simply too great for medicine to turn away from it. 99

—James D. Watson with Andrew Berry, *DNA: The Secret of Life.* New York: Knopf, 2003.

Watson, along with Francis Crick, discovered the structure of the DNA molecule, and along with Maurice Wilkins, received the Nobel Prize for Physiology or Medicine in 1962. Berry is a fruit fly geneticist and a research associate at Harvard University's Museum of Comparative Zoology.

Is Genetic Engineering Safe in Humans?

- The Human Genome Project, a 13-year effort to map the complete sequence of the **3 billion** DNA bases and identify all the human genes, finished two years ahead of schedule in 2003.

- The number of human genes was originally estimated to be **100,000**. Upon completion of the Human Genome Project in 2003, the number was lowered to 30,000 to 35,000, and was reduced again in 2004 to **20,000 to 24,000**.

- By 1970, **1,500 genetically determined diseases** had been identified in humans.

- **Genetic diseases** in which a single gene is responsible—the kind that would be most easily treated by gene therapy—are rare.

- By 2000 more than **500 gene therapy trials** on more than 4,000 patients had been registered with the NIH.

- **Viruses** have a natural ability to penetrate the host cell and express their viral genes. Scientists have harnessed this ability by genetically engineering viruses, inserting therapeutic genes into the virus, and then injecting the genetically engineered virus into the host, where the therapeutic gene is expressed.

Gene Therapy Using an Adenovirus

Adenovirus is a family of DNA viruses that is used as a vehicle for the delivery of genes in many forms of gene therapy. This illustrates gene therapy using an adenovirus vector (a disabled virus that is used to transmit DNA into the host). A new gene is inserted into an adenovirus vector, which is used to introduce the modified DNA into a human cell. If the treatment is successful, the new gene will make a functional protein.

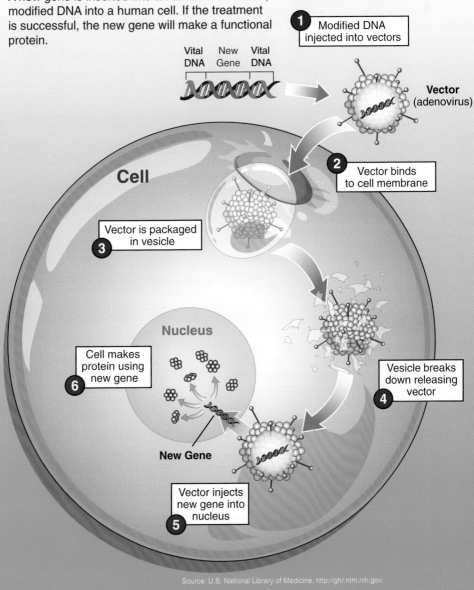

1 Modified DNA injected into vectors

Vital DNA   New Gene   Vital DNA

Vector (adenovirus)

2 Vector binds to cell membrane

Cell

3 Vector is packaged in vesicle

Nucleus

6 Cell makes protein using new gene

New Gene

4 Vesicle breaks down releasing vector

5 Vector injects new gene into nucleus

Source: U.S. National Library of Medicine. http://ghr.nlm.nih.gov.

Genetic Knowledge Quiz

In face-to-face interviews of more than 700 adults, most had heard about genetically modified foods and cloning, but few were aware of genetic therapy techniques. Moreover, while most had a basic knowledge about genetics, few were able to correctly answer more detailed questions about genetics. The results are listed below.

Note: correct answers in red

Statement	True	False	Don't Know
Identical twins have the same genes	65%	17%	18%
Whether a couple have a boy or a girl depends on the woman's genes	15%	64%	21%
Half your genes come from your mother and half from your father	61%	19%	20%
Down's syndrome is an inherited disease	22%	58%	20%
Children look like their parents because they have the same type of red blood cells	15%	58%	26%
Most cells in our body contain a copy of all our genes	57%	7%	36%
There are test-tube babies who grew entirely outside the mother's body	31%	47%	23%
Genes of all living things on Earth are made up of different combinations of only 4 or 5 chemical building blocks	28%	12%	61%
We have around 150,000 different chromosomes, which contain our genes	31%	13%	56%

Source: The Welcome Trust, "What Do People Think About Gene Therapy?" August 2005. www.welcome.ac.uk.

- Many **genetic disorders** are caused not by the absence of a gene, but by the presence of a faulty gene.

- Incorporating **foreign DNA** into a cell's genome is left up to chance. There is no way to control where the new DNA ends up.

Fundamentals of Gene Therapy

Deep in the nucleus of every cell are chromosomes that hold genes, composed of DNA (deoxyribonucleic acid), the building blocks of all organisms. When DNA is damaged, the result is disease or a disability. To cure a disease caused by genetic damage, researchers isolate normal genes and insert it into a vector, such as a disabled virus. Doctors then inject the vectors into diseased tissue. The vectors release the normal genes, thus restoring the diseased cells to normal.

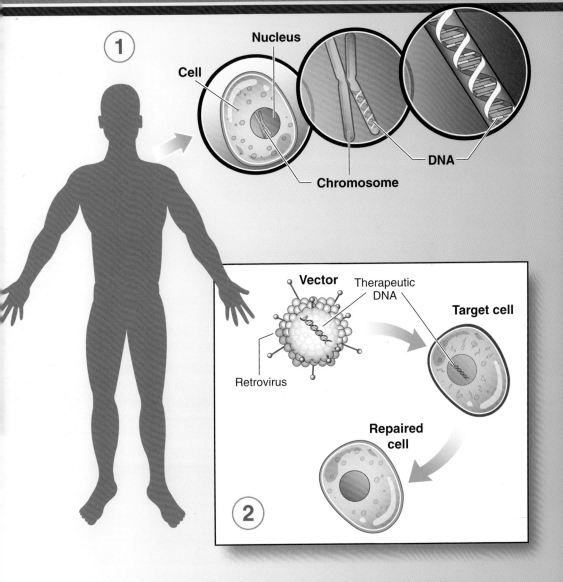

Source: Food and Drug Administration, "Fundamentals of Gene Therapy," August 14, 2000. www.fda.gov.

The Approval Rates of Gene Therapy Applications Are High

Surveys show strong support for gene therapy—even germ-line therapy—to prevent or cure diseases. However, there is less support for gene therapy for nonmedical uses.

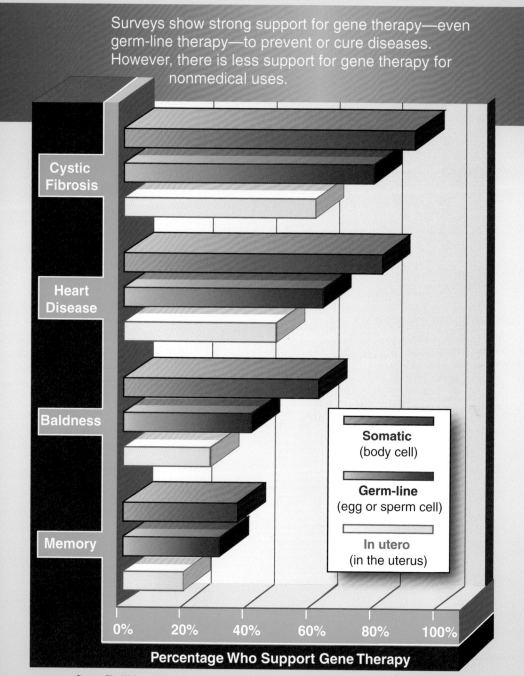

Cystic Fibrosis

Heart Disease

Baldness

Memory

Somatic
(body cell)

Germ-line
(egg or sperm cell)

In utero
(in the uterus)

0%   20%   40%   60%   80%   100%

Percentage Who Support Gene Therapy

Source: The Welcome Trust, "What Do People Think About Gene Therapy?" August 2005. www.welcome.ac.uk.

Americans Believe Reproductive Genetic Technology Will Lead to Designer Babies

Three-quarters of survey respondents agreed or strongly agreed with the statement that "Reproductive genetic technology will inevitably lead to genetic enhancement and designer babies." Participants were clear that it is not the technologies themselves that people fear, but rather that unrestrained human selfishness and vanity will drive people to use reproductive genetic testing inappropriately. They believe that the technology is being developed for good purposes, but human vices will result in consumer demand for capricious uses.

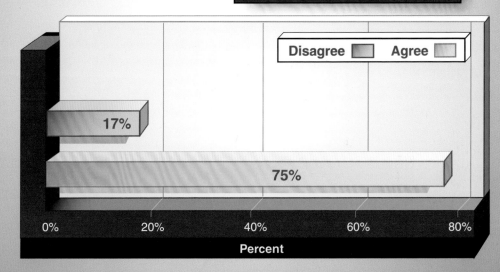

Percent who agreed with the statement "reproductive genetic technology will inevitably lead to genetic enhancement and designer babies."

Disagree | Agree

17%

75%

0%   20%   40%   60%   80%

Percent

Source: Genetics and Public Policy Center, "Reproductive Genetic Testing: America Thinks," December 2004. www.pewtrust.org.

- Although at least **10 other patients died** during gene therapy trials in the late 1990s, Jesse Gelsinger, an 18-year-old who died in September 1999, was the first publicly acknowledged death during a gene therapy trial. Doctors maintain that the other patients died not because of the gene therapy, but because they were **seriously ill**. Another death during a gene therapy trial was reported in July 2007.

- Gene therapy appeared to cure baby boys with severe combined immunodeficiency during the late 1990s. The babies were injected with **genetically engineered bone marrow** and improved enough to leave their sterile bubbles three months later. However, about two to three years later, two boys developed leukemia, and one died. The trials were halted.

- The **World Anti-Doping Agency** is working with researchers to develop a test to determine if athletes have injected themselves with genetic material that could enhance their athletic performance. EPO, a protein that enhances red blood cell production and increases oxygen delivery in the body, could give athletes a boost to their stamina and therefore a competitive edge to their performance.

Is Human Cloning Ethical?

> 66 Whether one clones an embryo for birth, or clones an embryo for research, a clone is a clone is a clone. 99
>
> —Kathleen Parker, "Calling a Clone a Clone," 2006.

> 66 The view that a cloned embryo is a person is, however, wrong. There is a huge difference between a cloned cluster of embryonic cells in a petri dish that could yield disease cures and a baby. 99
>
> —Arthur L. Caplan, "Cloning Ethics: Separating the Science from the Fiction," 2003.

Neither cloning nor stem cell research would be possible today if it were not for the advances made with in vitro fertilization during the 1970s. The first "test-tube baby," Louise Brown, was born in England in 1978, and the world was appalled at the time that an embryo was conceived outside the womb. Many believed that test-tube babies would be regarded as commodities and unloved. However, time has proved that view wrong. Since Louise Brown's birth, hundreds of thousands of couples have had test-tube babies, and most people now recognize that these babies are intensely wanted and loved and that in vitro fertilization is a blessing for infertile couples. So creating embryos in a petri dish is not new; what is new is what scientists are now doing with the knowledge: cloning embryos for research.

There are three types of genetically engineered human cloning. The first is molecular cloning, in which a DNA fragment is inserted into a bacterial plasmid that self-replicates, thus reproducing the DNA. The second is somatic cell nuclear transfer, also known as reproductive cloning, where the goal is to produce another human being that is genetically identical to its donor. The third is therapeutic cloning, in which human stem cells are cloned and used for research and medical treatments. Reproductive and therapeutic cloning are very similar procedures; the main difference between the two is that in therapeutic cloning, the embryos do not develop beyond the blastocyst stage. As of September 2007, reproductive cloning in humans had not been successful. Very few scientists, researchers, doctors, or ethicists support human reproductive cloning, and many nations have passed laws prohibiting the procedure.

How Cloning Works

A basic understanding of how reproductive and therapeutic cloning work is essential to understanding the issues involved in human cloning. In somatic cell nuclear transfer, the nucleus from a somatic cell (a specialized adult cell, such as a skin cell) is inserted into an egg cell that has had its nucleus removed. The egg cell with the transplanted nucleus is then stimulated with chemicals or electricity, which starts cell division.

Human Reproductive Cloning

When reproductive cloning is the goal, the embryo with the somatic cell nucleus is inserted in a womb, where it continues to grow and develop until its birth. Somatic cell nuclear transfer was the process used to produce Dolly, a Finn Dorset sheep that was the first mammal cloned from an adult cell. Until Dolly, scientists believed that mammals were too complex to be cloned. Cloning Dolly was not easy, however; it took 277 attempts before scientists had a viable egg that resulted in a live birth. Although many animals have been cloned since Dolly, the procedure is still fraught with challenges, including a high mortality rate for the embryos. The President's Council on Bioethics, established by George W. Bush in 2001 to advise him on the ethics of cloning, argued in its 2002 report that the high failure rate involved in reproductive clon-

> **Very few scientists, researchers, doctors, or ethicists support human reproductive cloning.**

ing meant that "attempts to clone a human being would be unethical at this time due to safety concerns."[31] In addition, the report stated that the procedure could not be made safe. The researchers who cloned Dolly failed hundreds of times before they were successful; any attempt to clone humans with such a track record of failures is unthinkable, the council asserted. Furthermore, it maintained, "conducting experiments in an effort to make cloning-to-produce-children less dangerous would itself be an unacceptable violation of the norms of research ethics. There seems to be no ethical way to try to discover whether cloning-to-produce-children can become safe, now or in the future."[32]

> " Cloning would allow infertile couples to have their own children. "

The few people who support human reproductive cloning argue that cloning would allow infertile couples to have their own children, or, if they became infertile after having a child, they could clone their child and have a younger twin sibling, a concept that Julian Savulescu endorses. Savulescu, who is the Uehiro professor of practical ethics at Oxford University, argues that no child has a right to genetic individuality, as some opponents claim. "Where does a 'right to genetic individuality' come from?" he asks. Savulescu notes that identical twins, who are natural clones, are considered "ordinary and autonomous individuals." As for the claim that cloned children would suffer unrealistic expectations of their abilities from their parents, cloning advocates maintain that many parents already have such expectations of their naturally born children. According to Savulescu:

> The role of the cloned child's parents would be the same as all of these parents': to love the child and give it a good upbringing. Whether clones have good or bad lives simply depends on society and how we choose to treat them, not on the facts of their DNA. We should not fear cloning technology, but instead should use it rationally and responsibly. And we should continue to treat other people, including clones, when they arrive, with equal concern and respect, making sure others also do the same.[33]

Savulescu concludes that if reproductive cloning becomes safe, with a high rate of success, there is no moral reason to ban it.

Embryonic Stem Cell Research

Therapeutic cloning is also known as embryo cloning, since the procedure clones embryonic cells. Researchers take a fertilized egg, allow it to divide for five days, then extract the stem cells from the embryos. The stem cell extraction kills the embryo, which many people object to for ethical reasons. The cloned embryonic cells are used in stem cell research in an attempt to treat certain diseases such as cancer, Parkinson's, Alzheimer's, and heart disease. These diseases may have diseased or faulty genes in the patient's cells that the scientists can study and use in their research. In addition, scientists hope one day to use therapeutic cloning to reproduce an entire organ for transplant into an ill patient or to repair damaged tissues.

Therapeutic cloning can also use adult stem cells, which are cells from a person's umbilical cord, skin, bone or bone marrow, and blood, for example. This technique does not use embryos and so is less controversial than embryonic stem cell research. Adult stem cells are actually already being used in clinical trials and have successfully treated sick patients. Two British scientists announced in October 2006 that they grew miniature human livers (about the size of a dime) in a laboratory from umbilical cord blood. The livers are an important first step in developing full-size livers, which the scientists estimate will not happen for about another 10 years. On the other hand, the long-promised spectacular results from embryonic stem cell research have yet to happen, notes Wesley J. Smith, a senior fellow at the Discovery Institute and a consultant to the Center for Bioethics and Culture. "Embryonic stem cells have not treated a single human patient, and only time can tell whether they ever will,"[34] he writes. Smith contends that such lack of progress shows that embryonic

> Cloned embryonic cells are used in stem cell research in an attempt to treat certain diseases such as cancer, Parkinson's, Alzheimer's, and heart disease.

stem cell research looks "more like a pipe dream than a realistic hope."[35]

However, some researchers claim that embryonic stem cells, which have not differentiated yet into specific cells as adult stem cells have, show more promise in treating and curing diseases than adult cells.

Christopher Reeve, an actor who was paralyzed in a fall from a horse and became an advocate for stem cell research, testified before the U.S. Senate about the importance of continuing research with embryonic stem cells. "Implantation of human embryonic stem cells is not safe unless they contain the patient's own

> **Therapeutic and reproductive cloning present issues that are frightening to many people.**

DNA," he told the senators. Furthermore, he continued, the research is ethical because the "therapeutic cloning is done without fertilizing an egg. It can be strictly regulated. If we also enforce an absolute ban on reproductive cloning, we will not slide down the dreaded slippery slope into moral and ethical chaos." Moreover, he added, it is the government's duty to encourage embryonic stem cell research. "Our government is supposed to do the greatest good for the greatest number of people."[36] According to Reeve, the greatest good for the greatest number of people means allowing embryonic stem cell research, which has the potential to help 150 million Americans who suffer from serious or incurable diseases or disabilities.

The "Human Embryo Is a Human Life" Argument

Many people oppose therapeutic cloning research that produces and uses embryonic stem cells. Since the first step in creating embryos for therapeutic cloning is the same as creating an embryo for reproductive cloning, many people fear that permitting human embryonic research will lead to attempts to clone humans. Charles Krauthammer, a member of the President's Council of Bioethics, explains in a statement he gave to other council members why he opposes research into therapeutic cloning:

> Research cloning is an open door to reproductive cloning.
> Banning the production of cloned babies while permit-

ting the production of cloned embryos makes no sense. If you have factories all around the country producing embryos for research and commerce, it is inevitable that someone will implant one in a woman (or perhaps in some artificial medium in the farther future) and produce a human clone.[37]

Currently in the United States no federal laws ban human reproductive cloning, although federal regulations prohibit funding research in human cloning. Since most scientists depend upon federal grants to fund their research, the federal ban effectively limits such research.

Many religious conservatives believe that life begins at conception. Thus for them a human embryo is a human life, and destroying the embryo to produce stem cells is tantamount to murder. Alfred Cioffi is a Catholic priest, a research ethicist for the National Catholic Bioethics Center, and an associate professor of bioethics and moral theology at Saint Vincent de Paul Regional Seminary in West Palm Beach, Florida. He has strong views about the morality of cloning—both reproductive and therapeutic. He writes, "The distinction between these two types of cloning is a biotechnical distinction without a moral difference; both are a crass manipulation of the intrinsic dignity of human life." Furthermore, he contends, all human life—no matter at what stage—is valuable, and to destroy it, even to save another life, devalues it. "It is never permissible to kill an innocent human life, even if this is done for the very noble cause of trying to cure the illness of someone else." There is no moral difference, he concludes, between reproductive cloning and therapeutic cloning. "The distinction in types of cloning is without a moral difference. Therapeutic cloning is extremely immoral just because the human embryo created in the lab is then sectioned into pieces in order to obtain stem cells."[38]

Ethical Dimensions

Therapeutic and reproductive cloning present issues that are frightening to many people. Just as the appearance of test-tube babies in the 1970s concerned many people who worried about the ethical implications of being able to conceive a child outside of the womb, so too does the development of cloning and stem cell research trouble those who worry whether the benefits outweigh the risks and harms.

Is Human Cloning Ethical?

66 Pluripotent [embryonic] stem cells offer the possibility of a renewable source of replacement cells and tissues to treat a myriad of diseases, conditions, and disabilities including Parkinson's and Alzheimer's diseases, spinal cord injury, stroke, burns, heart disease, diabetes, osteoarthritis and rheumatoid arthritis.99

—National Institutes of Health, "Stem Cells and Diseases," U.S. Department of Health and Human Services, 2007. http://stemcells.nih.gov.

The National Institutes of Health is the government's primary agency for the support of biomedical research and is responsible for developing guidelines for stem cell research.

66 It's not the cloned child that strikes fear into our hearts. Rather it's the idea that human beings could be designed to serve another's ends, to do another's bidding, to be controlled like a puppet on a string.99

—Arlene Judith Klotzko, *A Clone of Your Own? The Science and Ethics of Cloning.* New York: Cambridge University Press, 2006.

Klotzko, a bioethicist and a lawyer, is the author of *A Clone of Your Own? The Science and Ethics of Cloning.*

Bracketed quotes indicate conflicting positions.

* Editor's Note: While the definition of a primary source can be narrowly or broadly defined, for the purposes of Compact Research, a primary source consists of: 1) results of original research presented by an organization or researcher; 2) eyewitness accounts of events, personal experience, or work experience; 3) first-person editorials offering pundits' opinions; 4) government officials presenting political plans and/or policies; 5) representatives of organizations presenting testimony or policy.

❝Patients suffering from a whole host of afflictions—including (but not limited to) Parkinson's disease, autoimmune diseases, stroke, anemia, cancer, immunodeficiency, corneal damage, blood and liver diseases, heart attack, and diabetes—have experienced improved function following administration of therapies derived from adult or umbilical cord blood stem cells.❞

—Linda K. Bevington, "Stem Cell Research and 'Therapeutic' Cloning: A Christian Analysis," Center for Bioethics and Human Dignity, April 2005. www.cbhd.org.

Bevington is director of research at the Center for Bioethics and Human Dignity in Bannockburn, Illinois.

❝Cloning for research presents a new evil not found even in the practice of abortion: creating new human lives solely in order to destroy them.❞

—Richard M. Doerflinger, "Human Cloning vs. Human Dignity," U.S. Conference of Catholic Bishops. www.usccb.org.

Doerflinger is deputy director of the U.S. Conference of Catholic Bishops Secretariat for Pro-Life Activities.

❝Therapeutic cloning could *save* lives; it does not *create* people.❞

—Coalition for the Advancement of Medical Research, "FAQ on SCNT (Therapeutic Cloning)," www.stemcellfunding.org.

The Coalition for the Advancement of Medical Research is a coalition of patients, universities, researchers, and foundations that supports research into somatic cell nuclear transfer (therapeutic cloning) and opposes any attempts at reproductive human cloning.

❝Reproductive cloning will enable all of us to live eternally.❞

—Brigitte Boisselier, "Human Cloning Discussion at the UN," Clonaid, October 21, 2004. www.clonaid.com.

Boisselier is the scientific director of Clonaid, a company dedicated to creating human clones.

❝It is predictable that cloned children—as products of ethically dubious asexual reproduction—will be viewed by some as inferior, much the way that many people once looked down on children born out of wedlock.❞

—John F. Kilner and Robert P. George, "Human Cloning: What's at Stake," October 8, 2004. www.cbhd.org.

Kilner is president and chief executive officer of the Center for Bioethics and Human Dignity and Franklin Forman chair of ethics at Trinity International University in Deerfield, Illinois. George is McCormick Professor of Jurisprudence and director of the James Madison Program in American Ideals and Institutions at Princeton University, and a member of the President's Council on Bioethics.

❝Human embryos in dishes are not people or even potential people. They are, at best, *possible* potential people.❞

—Arthur L. Caplan, "Does Stem Cell Advance Provide an Ethical Out?" *MSNBC.com*, June 6, 2007. www.msnbc.com.

Caplan is director of the Center for Bioethics at the University of Pennsylvania.

❝If some members of our species can be deemed unworthy of respect and, therefore, cannibalized for science, why not other members?❞

—C. Ben Mitchell, "Clones from Newcastle," Center for Bioethics and Human Dignity, August 20, 2004. www.cbhd.org.

Mitchell is a senior fellow of the Center for Bioethics and Human Dignity and teaches bioethics at Trinity International University's Trinity Evangelical Divinity School in Deerfield, Illinois. He is also the bioethics consultant for the Ethics and Religious Liberty Commission of the Southern Baptist Convention.

❝To say that creating a clone is an affront to human dignity is like saying that deliberately creating a black person, or a woman, affronts human dignity.❞

—Julian Savulescu, "Equality, Cloning, and Clonism: Why We Must Clone," Reproductive Cloning Network. www.reproductivecloning.net.

Savulescu is Uehiro professor of practical ethics at the University of Oxford, director of the Oxford Uehiro Centre for Practical Ethics, and head of the Melbourne-Oxford Stem Cell Collaboration. He is also the editor of the *Journal of Medical Ethics* and the author of *Enhancement of Human Beings, Medical Ethics and the Law,* and *Ethical Issues in Genetic Research.*

❝Any attempt to clone a child would constitute not simply an unsafe procedure, but also a violation of internationally recognized rules on human experimentation.❞

—Marcy Darnovsky, "The Misstep of Human Cloning," *San Francisco Chronicle*, January 6, 2003.

Darnovsky is the associate executive director of the Center for Genetics and Society.

❝Stem cell research to cure debilitating diseases, using seven-day-old blastocysts, cloned or uncloned, is a noble exercise of our human ingenuity to promote healing.❞

—Michael J. Sandel, "Statement of Professor Sandel," in President's Council on Bioethics, *Human Cloning and Human Dignity: An Ethical Inquiry.* Washington, DC: President's Council on Bioethics, 2002.

Sandel, a professor of government at Harvard University, is a member of the President's Council on Bioethics and the author of *The Case Against Perfection: Ethics in the Age of Genetic Enhancement.*

Is Human Cloning Ethical?

- **Identical twins** are clones of each other.

- In 1978 the first **"test-tube baby,"** Louise Brown, was born in England. It is due to advances in the technology of in vitro fertilization that cloning and stem cell research are now possible.

- In **somatic cell nuclear transfer**, the nucleus of a somatic cell (a body cell that is not an egg or sperm) is inserted into an enucleated egg cell. The goal is to develop stem cells that will not be rejected by the patient's immune system.

- A **stem cell line** is a colony of stem cells that can replicate themselves in an artificial environment indefinitely.

- George W. Bush issued an executive order in 2001 that prohibited institutions that receive government grants for **stem cell research from establishing new stem cell lines**. Researchers who received federal funding could only work with stem cell lines that were in existence at the time of his executive order.

- In 2001 the government estimated there were **60 to 70 stem cell lines available for research**. As of September 2007 the NIH listed a registry of only 21 stem cell lines.

Reproductive and Therapeutic Cloning

Somatic cell nuclear transfer can create clones for both reproductive and therapeutic purposes; in practice, usually the whole donor cell is transferred.

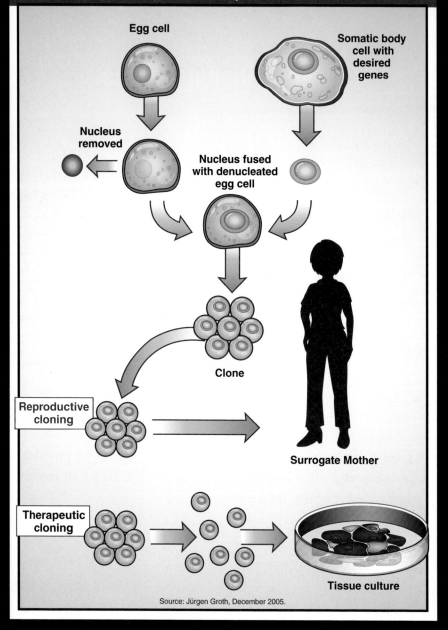

Source: Jürgen Groth, December 2005.

Americans' Support of Embryonic Stem Cell Research Vacillates

A poll of 1,000 adults in November 2006 found that the percentage who support embryonic stem cell research fell to 54 percent, down 4 percent from the previous year. Yet when the question was brought to a more personal level, 70 percent said they would support embryonic stem cell research in order to pursue treatment for themselves or their family members, up from 68 percent in 2005.

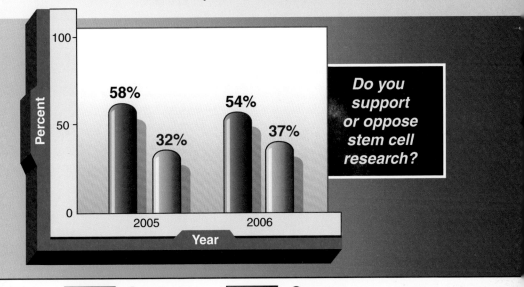

Do you support or oppose stem cell research?

58%   32%   54%   37%

Support   Oppose

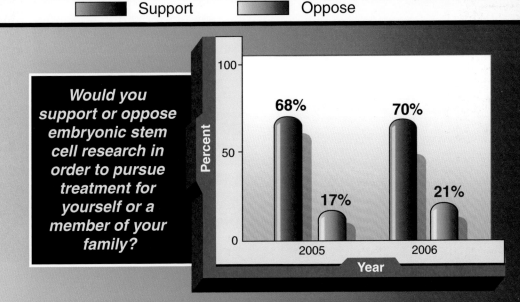

Would you support or oppose embryonic stem cell research in order to pursue treatment for yourself or a member of your family?

68%   17%   70%   21%

Source: Virginia Commonwealth University, Life Sciences Survey, "Opinions Shifting on Stem Cell Research, Opposition to Cloning Continues," 2006. www.vcu.edu.

Americans Oppose Human Cloning

A 2006 poll shows overwhelming opposition to human cloning, whether to provide children for infertile couples or to produce embryos that would be destroyed in medical research.

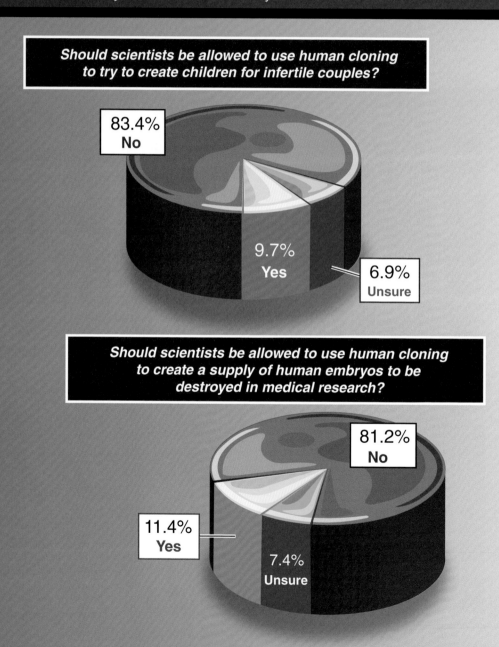

Should scientists be allowed to use human cloning to try to create children for infertile couples?

83.4%
No

9.7%
Yes

6.9%
Unsure

Should scientists be allowed to use human cloning to create a supply of human embryos to be destroyed in medical research?

81.2%
No

11.4%
Yes

7.4%
Unsure

Source: U.S. Conference of Catholic Bishops, "New Poll: Americans Continue to Oppose Funding Stem Cell Research That Destroys Human Embryos," May 31, 2006. www.usccb.org.

Stem Cells Rally Help for Hearts

Researchers injected stem cells into the hearts of laboratory rats and pigs that had suffered heart attacks and whose hearts were only pumping out 10 percent of the blood in their hearts. In humans, such a low percentage would require a heart transplant. The injection of genetically engineered stem cells into pigs and rats raised the percentage of blood pumped to 35–36 percent—still very low—compared to a normal human rate of 50–70 percent, but a dramatic improvement and one that appears to show that engineered stem cells are rallying more cells to come to the aid of the ailing heart cells. Researchers hope to start testing the stem cell treatment on humans in 2007.

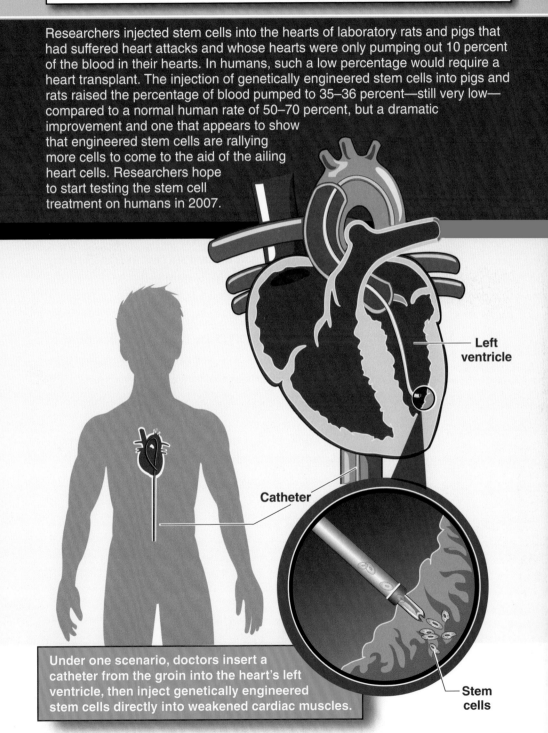

Left ventricle

Catheter

Stem cells

Under one scenario, doctors insert a catheter from the groin into the heart's left ventricle, then inject genetically engineered stem cells directly into weakened cardiac muscles.

Source: *Heart Advisor*, vol. 10, no. 12, p. 3, February 2007. www.heart-advisor.com.

73

- In a controversial experiment in 2004, doctors in Portugal **removed nasal cells from seven patients with spinal cord injuries** and transplanted them into the injured spinal cords. All the patients regained some motor function and sensation.

- If human cloning were attempted, it would be done through in vitro fertilization, which has only a **20 percent** success rate.

- Woo-suk Hwang, a South Korean biomedical scientist, claimed in 2004 that he had **cloned human embryos** and derived embryonic stem cells from them. His results were later proven to be falsified.

- **Embryonic stem cells used in research are from excess fertilized eggs** at fertility clinics and are donated for research by the infertile couples.

- **A scientist at Tokyo University** has had limited success in transforming an adult cell—which has been fused with a stem cell—back into the undifferentiated state of a stem cell.

- **Stem cells from early-stage mice embryos** are distinctly different from human embryonic stem cells. However, scientists discovered in June 2007 that stem cells from a later stage of mice embryos are a near-perfect match for human cells.

- Patients with over **70 types** of diseases and injuries have benefited from treatments using adult stem cells.

What Policies Should Govern Genetic Engineering?

> ❝If we are to prevent an escalating and potentially cata-
> strophic spiral of human genetic modification, we will
> need global bans on both reproductive human cloning
> and inheritable genetic modification.❞
>
> —Center for Genetics and Society, "Introduction: The Minimal Critical Policy Regime," 2004.

> ❝Prohibition of enhancement technologies wouldn't
> stop people from seeking to use them any more than
> the War on Drugs has stopped people from seeking
> recreational chemicals.❞
>
> —Ramez Naam, *More than Human: Embracing the Promise of Biological Enhancement.* 2005.

Just as the issue of genetic engineering is contentious, so too is the role the government should play in regulating the science. Because genetic engineering covers the spectrum—from agriculture to the environment to health—so too does government oversight of genetic engineering. The government must determine what effect, if any, biotechnology will have on the environment, human health, social and economic conditions, and religious and moral values, and then it must decide what action it should take to protect those interests.

When the U.S. Patent and Trademark Office was established, its purpose was to award a patent protecting the inventor's right to manufacture or produce a mechanical, electrical, or chemical design or invention that was "useful," "novel," and "not obvious."[39] Since living organisms were a product of nature and were neither mechanical, electrical, or chemical inventions, they were exempt from patents. Inventors could patent a harvesting machine, but not the harvest. However, beginning in 1930 the patent office began awarding patents to plants that had been developed asexually (plants that reproduced through budding, grafting, rooting of clippings, or dividing bulbs). Some farmers and their advocates were upset when giant agricultural corporations began patenting the seed they sold to farmers. Once the agribusinesses patented the seeds, farmers could no longer save seed from their harvest to plant the following year. They had to buy new seed every year to plant their crops. And to ensure that farmers would not replant the seeds the following year, several agricultural corporations genetically engineered the seeds so that they cannot germinate when they are replanted. Camila Montecinos of the Chilean-based Center for Education and Technology said that such technology "robs farming communities of their age-old right to save seed and their role as plant breeders. It should be banned."[40]

> "The government must determine what effect, if any, biotechnology will have on the environment, human health, social and economic conditions, and religious and moral values, and then it must decide what action it should take to protect those interests."

The rules about what can and cannot be patented changed again in 1980, when the U.S. Supreme Court ordered the patent office to grant a patent on a bacterium that had been genetically engineered to clean up oil spills by eating the oil. In a 5-4 decision, the Court ruled that "whether the invention was alive or dead was irrelevant, . . . the bacterium was not a product of nature, . . . and hence deserved a patent."[41] Next came a patent in 1988 for genetically engineered mice. Researchers at Harvard University developed mice that had been genetically engineered to carry genes for breast cancer so that scientists could study cancer development and the effects of cancer drugs on the disease. Scientists who wished to work with the mice in their cancer research would have to pay a licensing fee to Harvard University.

Patenting Humans

Then in 1995 the NIH received the first patent for a person's unmodified genes. The DNA belonged to a man from an extremely small tribe known as the Hagahai in Papua New Guinea, which first came in contact with the Western world in 1984. The NIH was interested in the tribe's genes because the tribe members were resistant to a retrovirus that causes leukemia and lymphoma in humans. The NIH, which the patent office recognizes as the official owner of the tribe's cell line, argues that the tribe's cells are valuable because they could help researchers diagnose and treat diseases and develop vaccines.

The patent office's grant of this patent was quite controversial and raised questions over the ethics of assigning a commercial right to living entities and their genes and cells. Supporters of the patents argued that patents are necessary to keep important research going—the ability to patent intellectual property attracts and keeps investors who fund the research. In 2003, according to Dan Eramian, vice president at Biotechnology Industry Organization, a biotechnology trade organization, "Investors poured almost $17 billion into biotech companies, despite the fact that most have no products on the market and will probably lose money years before turning profitable. And many will never become profitable."[42] Yet investors continue to pour money into biotechnology companies because, he explains, the patents protect intellectual property, and if a project is successful, the investors will earn back their money. A patent appeals board ruled that patenting human genes is not "a form of modern slavery," nor does it "give the patent holder any rights over the person from whom the genes were taken."

> Once the agribusinesses patented the seeds, farmers could no longer save seed from their harvest to plant the following year.

Moreover, "the patenting of a single human gene has nothing to do with the patenting of a human life. Even if every gene in the human genome were cloned (and possibly patented) it would be impossible to reconstitute a human being from the sum of its genes."[43]

> **Supporters of the patents argued that patents are necessary to keep important research going— the ability to patent intellectual property attracts and keeps investors who fund the research.**

Patent opponents argue that patenting human genes for profit is immoral, offends human dignity, and is synonymous with patenting human life. Furthermore, patents keep other scientists from pursuing similar research, or convince them to perform their research in secret so they do not have to pay licensing fees. Opponents assert that such actions—or lack of actions—thus disrupt the collaboration that is traditional between private and public researchers. In addition, not all countries agree that it is ethical to patent these organisms. The Canadian Patent Office rejected the patent on Harvard mice, and the European Patent Office rejected the patent on the Hagahai tribe's genes. An official with the Papua New Guinea government asks, "Can this cell line truly be the intellectual property of the U.S. government and the scientists, when the property was derived, alienated from a citizen of PNG?"[44] For her part, the U.S. researcher who helped obtain the patent says she will return any royalties and licensing fees to the Hagahai tribe.

Cloning

Around the same time as the isolation and the patenting of the Hagahai man's DNA, another biotechnology discovery caused an uproar. Scientists at the Roslin Institute in Edinburgh, Scotland, led by Ian Wilmut, announced in 1997 that they had cloned a sheep from an adult mammary cell. Dolly was the first mammal to be cloned via somatic cell nuclear transfer. Since Dolly's birth, scientists have cloned numerous other animals via somatic cell nuclear transfer, from mice to endangered species.

The announcement of Dolly's existence brought about immediate calls for banning all forms of cloning. President Bill Clinton, while acknowledging that cloning holds much promise for advances in crops, livestock, and medical treatments, asserted that the new knowledge also presented a heavy responsibility for science and society.

> The recent breakthrough in animal cloning is one that could yield enormous benefits, enable us to reproduce the most productive strains of crop and livestock, holding out the promise of revolutionary new medical treatments and cures, helping to unlock the greatest secrets of the genetic code. But like the splitting of the atom, this is a discovery that carries burdens as well as benefits.[45]

The president then issued a directive banning the use of federal funds for research on human cloning. While he could only restrict federal funds for cloning research, he urged the scientific community to follow a voluntary moratorium on private cloning research. Most governments and biotechnology researchers around the world agreed that human reproductive cloning was morally repugnant and prohibited the research.

Despite the nearly universal ban on human cloning, a few maverick scientists announced that they would attempt to clone—or had successfully cloned—a human baby. Richard Seed and Severino Antinori announced they would conduct human cloning experiments. By 2002 several researchers—a South Korean company; Clonaid, a Canadian biotechnology company founded by a UFO cult; and Panayiotis Zavos, a Greek fertility researcher—announced that they had implanted cloned embryos in women. Clonaid reported further success with cloned human embryos in the next few years. None of these claims were ever verified by outside sources.

> " Patent opponents argue that patenting human genes for profit is immoral, offends human dignity, and is synonymous with patenting human life. "

Although most countries have banned cloning for reproductive purposes, many allow cloning for therapeutic reasons, such as research on curing or treating diseases. In therapeutic cloning, researchers take the nucleus from a patient's adult cell and insert it into an egg cell that has had its nucleus removed. After the cell starts dividing, scientists separate the embryo into individual cells. This separation of the embryonic cells kills the embryo. Researchers then extract stem cells (which can develop into any type of cell in the body, such as blood, bone, skin, brain, and so forth) from the individual cells. Scientists believe that inserting or injecting the patient's own stem cells back into his or her body starts repairing the damaged cells, thus curing the disease. Many scientists are excited by the possibilities of embryonic stem cell research because these stem cells are a genetic match to the patient, and so the body should not reject them.

The embryos used in therapeutic cloning can also be taken from leftover embryos from fertility clinics, since many of the embryos are discarded after a couple achieves a successful pregnancy. But despite the promise of stem cell research, many people oppose this method, insisting that it is immoral because the very act of extracting the stem cells from the embryo kills a human life. Concerned about the destruction of human embryos for research purposes, President George W. Bush announced on August 9, 2001, that he was placing a moratorium on federal funds for research that involved destroying human embryos. In a televised speech, Bush said: "While we must devote enormous energy to conquering disease, it is equally important that we pay attention to the moral concerns raised by the new frontier of human embryo stem cell research. Even the most noble ends do not justify any means."[46] Under the new moratorium, Bush announced that scientists would still be able to do research on stem cell lines that had been created prior to August 9, 2001, but the federal government would no longer provide funds for any research on embryonic stem cells. (A stem cell line is a colony of stem cells that has been created from an embryo and has been continuously regenerated.)

New Regulations

While research on cloned and embryonic stem cells had not been banned completely, the new regulations make research much more difficult to pursue. Human embryos can still be cloned and embryonic stem cell lines can still be created, but only if all funding is from sources other than the federal government. The president's August 9, 2001, directive means a researcher cannot perform research on human embryonic cloning or human embryos if the building, the equipment, or the employees have been paid with federal funds. So many scientists who want to pursue such research must set up entire new laboratories, all paid for with nonfederal funds.

Several states have stepped up to provide funds or facilities for stem cell research. As of 2007, 9 states—California, Connecticut, Illinois, Indiana, Massachusetts, Maryland, New Jersey, New York, and Wisconsin—provide funding for stem cell research, while a tenth state, Missouri, passed a constitutional amendment in 2006 guaranteeing researchers and patients access to any stem cell research or treatment not prohibited by federal law. But building and paying for new facilities that are not under federal control means there is less state and private money available for actual research. According to the liberal U.S. think tank Center for American Progress, just 15 percent of state funding has been spent on actual stem cell research; 55 percent, or almost $425 million, has been spent on new infrastructure, equipment, training, and other expenses. While the Center for American Progress is glad for state support, it asserts that allowing the states—instead of the federal government—to be the driving force on stem cell research will lead to different regulations in each state, divergent research standards, and hamper collaborative research between scientists in different states because what is legal in one state may be illegal in another.

No Consensus

While politicians, ethicists, and most researchers seem content with a ban on reproductive cloning, there is no consensus on cloning for research purposes. Some legislators and ethicists support bans on research cloning, while others oppose such bans. After an attempt in 2002 to reach a compromise by imposing a moratorium on therapeutic cloning failed, Michael Werner of the Biotechnology Industy Organization said, "A moratorium on research is a ban on research, and that is not a compromise to us."[47] The result of a lack of consensus concerning cloning is that both research and therapeutic cloning are still legal under federal laws, with individual states making up their own—and contradictory—legislation.

What Policies Should Govern Genetic Engineering?

> **"Biotech crops are the most thoroughly regulated crops ever."**

—Martina Newell-McGloughlin, "Are Genetically Modified Crops Safe?" *Talk of the Nation*, May 5, 2006. www.npr.org.

Newell-McGloughlin is the director of the University of California System-Wide Biotechnology Research and Energy Program.

> **"The question becomes . . . is the regulatory system here adequate to protect the public [from genetically modified crops], and we don't think it is."**

—Doug Gurian-Sherman, "Are Genetically Modified Crops Safe?" *Talk of the Nation*, May 5, 2006. www.npr.org.

Gurian-Sherman is a senior scientist for the Center for Food Safety, International Center for Technology Assessment in Washington, D.C.

Bracketed quotes indicate conflicting positions.

* Editor's Note: While the definition of a primary source can be narrowly or broadly defined, for the purposes of Compact Research, a primary source consists of: 1) results of original research presented by an organization or researcher; 2) eyewitness accounts of events, personal experience, or work experience; 3) first-person editorials offering pundits' opinions; 4) government officials presenting political plans and/or policies; 5) representatives of organizations presenting testimony or policy.

❝If we are going to ban such improvements [genetic enhancements] to our quality of life, we had better have strong evidence that the research poses a greater threat to society than the medical benefits it brings.❞

—Ramez Naam, *More than Human: Embracing the Promise of Biological Enhancement.* New York: Broadway, 2005.

Naam is the author of *More than Human: Embracing the Promise of Biological Enhancement.*

....

❝If a [genetically engineered] product looked like a pesticide, we're going to regulate it like a pesticide. If it looks like a food, we're going to regulate like a food. If it looks like a drug, we'll regulate it like a drug.❞

—Michael Fernandez, "Are Genetically Modified Crops Safe?" *Talk of the Nation*, May 5, 2006. www.npr.org.

Fernandez is the executive director of the Pew Initiative on Food and Biotechnology, a think tank in Washington, D.C.

....

❝As genetic sciences and biotechnology developed, the federal regulatory agencies were taken somewhat by surprise. The agencies did not have the background or expertise to regulate the new varieties of crop plants that were being developed, and they did not have the background to regulate the environmental impacts of transgenic crops in agriculture.❞

—Roger Beachy, "The Genomic Revolution: Everything You Wanted to Know About Plant Genetic Engineering but Were Afraid to Ask," *Bulletin of the American Academy of Arts and Sciences*, Spring 2002.

Beachy is the founding president and director of the Donald Danforth Plant Science Center in St. Louis, Missouri. He is known internationally for his research on developing virus-resistant plants through biotechnology.

....

"Safety is not at issue in labeling biotech food."

—Council for Biotechnology Information, "Biotech Labeling," www.whybiotech.com.

The Council for Biotechnology Information is composed of leading biotechnology companies and trade associations who educate the public about the safety of agricultural and food biotechnology.

....

"Unlike other developed countries, we have not been informed that almost 70% of our corn, 90% of our soy and 75% of our processed food now contain neurotoxins, novel proteins and allergens."

—Robyn O'Brien, "Our Intimate Relationship with Food: A Complex Truth," August 20, 2007. www.healthychild.org.

O'Brien is the founder of AllergyKids, an organization devoted to raising awareness about food allergies and children.

....

"States lack the revenue, infrastructure, and incentives to properly promote stem cell research on their own, especially with federal policies that limit collaboration, impede their funding, and fail to provide regulatory guidelines."

—Sam Berger, "Keep the Focus on the Feds," April 27, 2007. www.bioethicsforum.org.

Berger is a researcher at the Center for American Progress Action Fund, a progressive think tank that believes the government should champion the common good over narrow self-interest.

....

"We are not creating or patenting human beings, or creepy critters, but life-saving technologies like vaccines, drugs and crops that can deliver better yields. Patents help our member companies fund the research and development for these technologies."

—Dan Eramian, "Patents Save Lives," Speech to the Global Public Policy Institute and Ecole de Science Politique, June 24, 2004.

Eramian is the former vice president of communications at the Biotechnology Industy Organization, a biotechnology lobbying group in Washington, D.C.

....

"The hasty patenting of human genes really does affect the entire development of drugs and vaccines."

—Greenpeace, "The True Cost of Gene Patents: The Economic and Social Consequences of Patenting Genes and Living Organisms," June 15, 2004. www.greenpeace.org.

Greenpeace is an international activist organization that opposes using genetic engineering in food, crops, and animals.

....

"Our failed stem cell policy has significantly hampered research in the U.S., and could have a detrimental effect on our efforts to find life-saving cures and remain the world leader in biomedical research."

—Jonathan Moreno, Sam Berger, and Alix Rogers, "Divided We Fail: The Need for National Stem Cell Funding: An Analysis of State and Federal Funding for Stem Cell Research," Center for American Progress, April 2007. www.americanprogress.org.

Moreno is a senior fellow at the Center for American Progress and director of the Progressive Bioethics Initiative. Berger is a research assistant at the Center for American Progress. Rogers was a bioethics intern at the Center for American Progress at the time this report was written.

....

66 Because of President Bush's restrictions, some of our best and brightest scientists are leaving the United States to work overseas in countries that have embraced the promise of comprehensive stem cell research. 99

—Dianne Feinstein, "Senator Feinstein Urges Passage of the Stem Cell Research Enhancement Act," July 17, 2006. http://feinstein.senate.gov.

Feinstein is a democratic senator from California.

66 American scientists are by far the world leaders in embryonic-stem-cell research—publishing 46 percent of all articles on the subject. 99

—Eric Cohen, "Stem-Cell Sense," *National Review Online*, May 25, 2006.

Cohen is the editor of the *New Atlantis* and director of the program on Bioethcis and American Democracy at the Ethics and Public Policy Center in Washington, D.C.

66 Frozen embryos in infertility clinics face a fate of certain destruction anyway. The moral case against using them, or cloned embryos, which have almost zero chance of becoming people, is no less compelling because progress has been made in another area of research. 99

—Arthur L Caplan, "Does Stem Cell Advance Provide an Ethical Out?" *MSNBC.com*, June 6, 2007. www.MSNBC.com.

Caplan is the director of the Center for Bioethics at the University of Pennsylvania School of Medicine and the chair of the department of medical ethics.

66 There's no such thing as excess life, and the fact that a living being is going to die does not justify experimenting on it or exploiting it as a natural resource. 99

—George W. Bush, "President Discusses Stem Cell Research," White House, August 9, 2001. www.whitehouse.gov.

Bush is the forty-third of the United States.

What Policies Should
Govern Genetic Engineering?

- The FDA and the NIH oversee the safety and effectiveness of gene therapy trials. **Gene therapy trials** are supposed to be approved before they can be attempted on humans.

- **Fifteen states have banned** all or some forms of human cloning.

- The U.S. Supreme Court ruled in 1980 that **living organisms could be patented**. The first patent was placed later that year on a genetically engineered single-celled bacterium developed to clean up oil spills.

- The U.S. Patent and Trademark Office accepted the **first patent on a genetically engineered mouse** in 1988. The mouse had been altered to be more susceptible to breast cancer.

- In 2002 the **Canadian Supreme Court refused** to allow patents on living organisms.

- More than **4,000 genes**—or about **20 percent** of human genes—had been patented in the United States as of 2005.

- **The U.S. government limits funding for stem cell research** to adult stem cells and a few lines of embryonic stem cells that were developed before August 9, 2001.

Countries' Policies on Embryonic Stem Cell Research

Countries colored brown have a permissive or flexible policy on human embryonic stem cell research. The brown countries represent about 3.5 billion people, more than 50 percent of the world's population.

Permissive policy allows various laboratory techniques to create embroynic stem cell lines, including nuclear transfer/research cloning and the extraction of stem cells from embryos that remain unused after IVF treatments.

Flexible policy allows the creation of stem cell lines from donated embryos unused after IVF treatments.

Restrictions or no established policies range from outright prohibition of human embryo research to permitting research on imported embryonic stem cell lines only to permitting research on a limited number of previously established stem cell lines.

Source: MBBNet.com, 2007.

- California voters passed **Proposition 71** in 2004 which provides $3 billion over 10 years for stem cell research. It is the largest state-supported scientific research program in the nation.

- The NIH regulates experiments on **human subjects**, including embryos and stem cells.

A Number of States Support Stem Cell Research

A number of states have chosen to attract embryonic stem cell research efforts by providing millions of dollars to support research that is not eligible for federal funds as determined by President George W. Bush's August 2001 stem cell research policy.

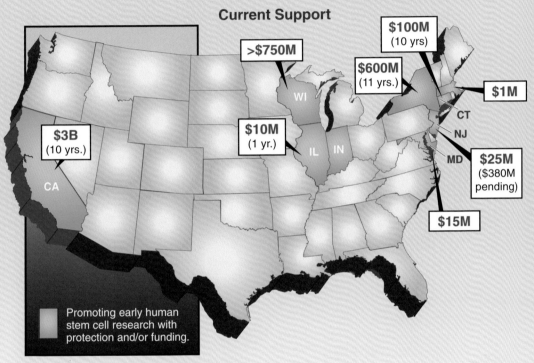

Current Support

$100M (10 yrs)

>$750M

$600M (11 yrs.)

$1M

WI

$3B (10 yrs.)

$10M (1 yr.)

CA

IL   IN

CT

NJ

MD $25M ($380M pending)

$15M

Promoting early human stem cell research with protection and/or funding.

Source: A. Mauron and M.E. Jaconi, "Stem Cell Science: Current Ethical and Policy Issues," 2007.

- Missouri residents passed **Amendment 2** in 2006, which prevents the state legislature from restricting treatment or research for embryonic stem cells that is permitted by federal law. However, the amendment prohibits human reproductive cloning.

- The NIH provides almost **75 percent** of all public funding to researchers for stem cell research. The NIH also provides **88 percent** of funding for embryonic stem cell research.

State Policies on Embryonic Stem Cell Research

While many states are trying to attract early embryonic stem cell research, approximately 10 states currently have restrictions in their state law that prohibits various forms of embryonic human stem cell research. The following map demonstrates current state policies that may limit embryonic stem cell research.

Current State Policies

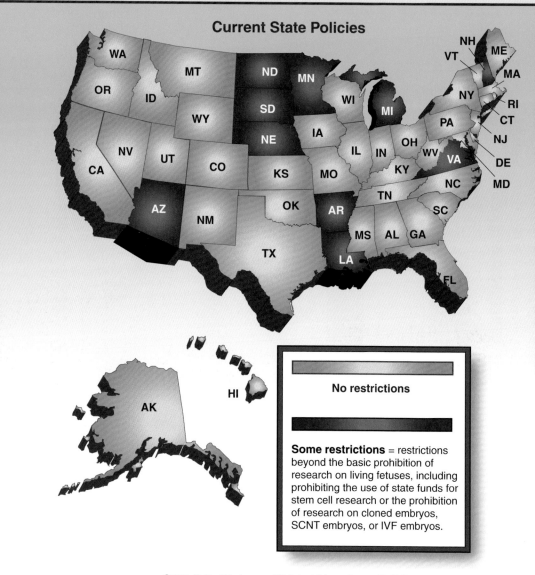

No restrictions

Some restrictions = restrictions beyond the basic prohibition of research on living fetuses, including prohibiting the use of state funds for stem cell research or the prohibition of research on cloned embryos, SCNT embryos, or IVF embryos.

Source: National Conference of State Legislatures, January 19, 2007. www.ncsl.org.

What Policies Should Govern Genetic Engineering?

For the second time, President George W. Bush vetoed a bill that would have expanded federal funding for embryonic stem cell research. Most Americans disapproved of his decision to veto the bill.

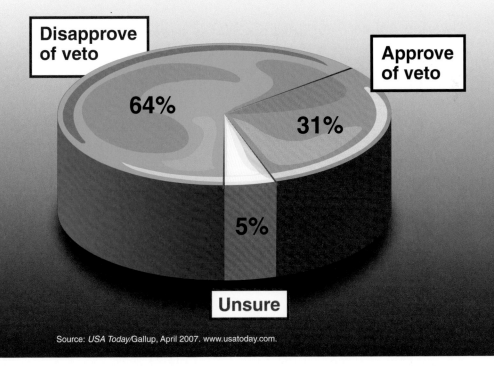

Disapprove of veto 64%

Approve of veto 31%

Unsure 5%

Source: *USA Today*/Gallup, April 2007. www.usatoday.com.

- At least **44 bills to ban human cloning** have been introduced into the U.S. Congress since 1997. None has been passed by both houses.

- **The Centers for Disease Control and Prevention** collects data on fertility clinics and in vitro fertilization.

Key People and Advocacy Groups

W. French Anderson: The former director of gene therapy at the University of Southern California Medical School, Anderson was the first person to attempt authorized somatic gene transfer experiments on humans by inserting healthy genes into Ashanti DeSilva, a four-year-old girl with severe combined immunodeficiency.

Severino Antinori: An Italian specialist in human fertility, Antinori has helped postmenopausal women give birth, including a 63-year-old woman in 1994 and a 62-year-old woman in 2006. He has also claimed to have cloned humans but has not provided proof.

Peter Beyer: Beyer is a plant biologist who, along with Ingo Potrykus, invented Golden Rice, a genetically engineered rice fortified with vitamin A.

Brigitte Boisselier: Boisselier is the chief executive officer of Clonaid and a Raëlian who claimed in 2002 that Clonaid had cloned a human baby. No proof was ever offered to support her claim.

Louise Brown: The world's first "test-tube baby," Brown was the result of in vitro fertilization, in which the egg is fertilized with sperm outside the womb, then transferred into the uterus with the hope it will implant itself and result in pregnancy.

Clonaid: Clonaid is a project established by Claude Vorilhon, now known as Raël, to clone human beings.

Francis Crick: Crick is the codiscoverer, along with James D. Watson, of the molecular structure of DNA. He received the Nobel Prize in 1962 for his work.

Dolly: A Finn Dorset sheep, Dolly was the first mammal to be cloned from an adult cell. Dolly developed arthritis at 5 years old, an unusually young age, and died in 2003 when she was 6, a very young age for a sheep. Some speculate that she may have been susceptible to premature aging due to the fact that her donor cell came from a 6-year-old sheep, theorizing that her cells were already 6 years old when she was born.

Golden Rice Project: This project is a private-public partnership established in 2001 between the inventors of Golden Rice, Ingo Potrykus and Peter Beyer, and the agricultural chemical manufacturer Syngenta. The project is developing Golden Rice, a strain of rice that has been genetically modified by inserting beta-carotene into its genes. The bio-fortified rice will be donated to farmers in developing countries where vitamin A deficiency is a serious problem in the population.

Human Genome Project: The Human Genome Project was an international project started in 1990 with the goal of identifying all the genes in the human genome and mapping how they are sequenced. The project, which finished two years ahead of schedule in 2003, discovered there are only between 20,000 and 25,000 genes in the human genome.

Woo-suk Hwang: Hwang is a Korean geneticist who claimed in 2004 that he was the first scientist to successfully clone a human embryo using somatic cell nuclear transfer techniques. However, in 2006 a South Korean academic panel determined that Hwang had faked his data and had not produced any cloned embryonic stem cell lines.

Karl Illmensee: A Swiss scientist, Illmensee claimed in 1979 that he had cloned mice. His results were not duplicated by any scientist until 1998.

Leon Kass: An American bioethicist known for his opposition to embryonic stem cell and cloning research, Kass is a member and former chair of the President's Council on Bioethics.

Gregor Mendel: Mendel was an Austrian monk who studied how certain traits were inherited by peas. His work became the foundation of the study of genetics.

Ingo Potrykus: Potrykus is a plant geneticist who, along with Peter Beyer, invented Golden Rice, a genetically engineered rice fortified with vitamin A.

President's Council on Bioethics: The council is a group of leading ethicists and researchers who advise the president on biomedical issues such as cloning, stem cell research, and gene therapy.

Raëlians: The Raëlians are a cult in which the followers claim that life on Earth was created by extraterrestrials. Its leader is Raël, formerly known as Claude Vorilhon, who is actively trying to clone humans.

Christopher Reeve: Reeve was an actor who portrayed Superman in three movies. He was paralyzed from the neck down after he was thrown from his horse in 1994. He became a staunch supporter of stem cell research to treat spinal cord injuries.

Roslin Institute: The Roslin Institute is a Scottish research facility where Ian Wilmut and his colleagues cloned Dolly, the first mammal cloned from an adult cell.

Davor Solter: An American scientist, Solter, along with his student Frank McGrath, was unsuccessful in repeating Karl Illmensee's experiment of cloning mice and declared in a 1984 article published by *Science* magazine that "the cloning of mammals by simple nuclear transfer is biologically impossible."

Hans Spemann: Spemann, a German embryologist and Nobel Prize laureate, is known as the "Father of Cloning." Working with Hilda Mangold, Spemann transferred the nucleus of a salamander embryo into another salamander cell in 1924, thus performing the first cloning experiment using the nuclear transfer method.

Craig Venter: Venter is a biologist who founded and is the former president of Celera Genomics, a company that was in a race with the Human Genome Project to identify and sequence the human genome.

James D. Watson: Along with Francis Crick, Watson discovered the structure of the DNA molecule. Watson, Crick, and molecular biologist Maurice Wilkins were awarded the Nobel Prize in 1962 for their DNA discoveries.

Irv Weissman: A pioneering researcher in the area of stem cells, Weissman is the director of Stanford's Institute for Cancer and Stem Cell Biology.

Ian Wilmut: Wilmut is a Scottish researcher who led the team of scientists who cloned Dolly, the first mammal to be cloned from an adult cell.

Panayiotis (Panos) Zavos: A former associate of Severino Antinori, Zavos is a leading scientist in stem cell research. He also claims to have cloned humans and has published photographs in national scientific magazines of what he says is a four-day-old cloned embryo.

Chronology

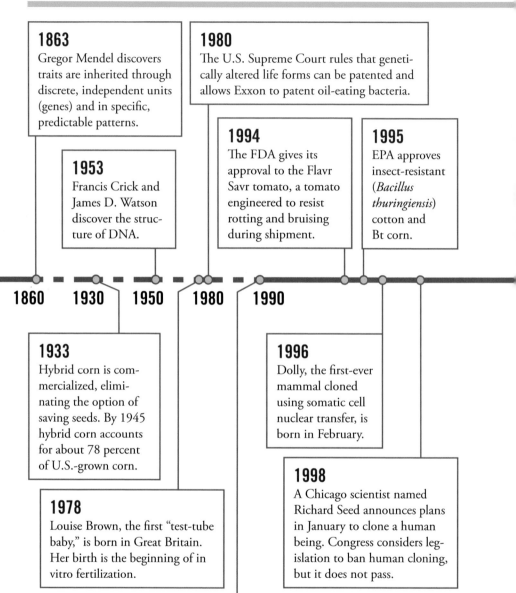

1863
Gregor Mendel discovers traits are inherited through discrete, independent units (genes) and in specific, predictable patterns.

1980
The U.S. Supreme Court rules that genetically altered life forms can be patented and allows Exxon to patent oil-eating bacteria.

1953
Francis Crick and James D. Watson discover the structure of DNA.

1994
The FDA gives its approval to the Flavr Savr tomato, a tomato engineered to resist rotting and bruising during shipment.

1995
EPA approves insect-resistant (*Bacillus thuringiensis*) cotton and Bt corn.

1860   1930   1950   1980   1990

1933
Hybrid corn is commercialized, eliminating the option of saving seeds. By 1945 hybrid corn accounts for about 78 percent of U.S.-grown corn.

1996
Dolly, the first-ever mammal cloned using somatic cell nuclear transfer, is born in February.

1998
A Chicago scientist named Richard Seed announces plans in January to clone a human being. Congress considers legislation to ban human cloning, but it does not pass.

1978
Louise Brown, the first "test-tube baby," is born in Great Britain. Her birth is the beginning of in vitro fertilization.

1988
The U.S. Patent and Trademark Office grants a patent on the OncoMouse, a transgenic mouse developed at Harvard University that had been altered to make the animal susceptible to breast cancer.

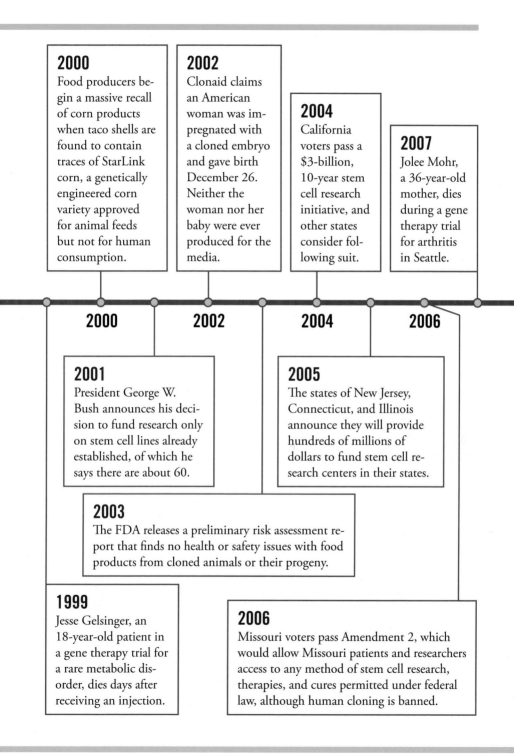

2000
Food producers begin a massive recall of corn products when taco shells are found to contain traces of StarLink corn, a genetically engineered corn variety approved for animal feeds but not for human consumption.

2002
Clonaid claims an American woman was impregnated with a cloned embryo and gave birth December 26. Neither the woman nor her baby were ever produced for the media.

2004
California voters pass a $3-billion, 10-year stem cell research initiative, and other states consider following suit.

2007
Jolee Mohr, a 36-year-old mother, dies during a gene therapy trial for arthritis in Seattle.

2000   2002   2004   2006

2001
President George W. Bush announces his decision to fund research only on stem cell lines already established, of which he says there are about 60.

2005
The states of New Jersey, Connecticut, and Illinois announce they will provide hundreds of millions of dollars to fund stem cell research centers in their states.

2003
The FDA releases a preliminary risk assessment report that finds no health or safety issues with food products from cloned animals or their progeny.

1999
Jesse Gelsinger, an 18-year-old patient in a gene therapy trial for a rare metabolic disorder, dies days after receiving an injection.

2006
Missouri voters pass Amendment 2, which would allow Missouri patients and researchers access to any method of stem cell research, therapies, and cures permitted under federal law, although human cloning is banned.

Related Organizations

Alliance for Bio-Integrity

2040 Pearl Ln. #2

Fairfield, IA 52556

phone: (206) 888-4582 • e-mail: info@biointegrity.org

Web site: www.biointegrity.org

The Alliance for Bio-Integrity is dedicated to the advancement of human and environmental health through sustainable and safe technologies. It advocates a more rational and prudent policy on genetically engineered foods, including mandatory testing and labeling of such foods. A variety of articles and reports, including the report *The Poor Performance of Genetically Engineered Crops*, is available on its Web site.

Biotechnology Industry Organization (BIO)

1225 I St. NW, Suite 400

Washington, DC 20005

phone: (202) 962-9200

e-mail: info@bio.org • Web site: www.bio.org

BIO is a trade association that represents hundreds of biotechnology companies. It champions biotechnology and advocates on behalf of its member organizations. The organization promotes the safety of genetically engineered foods and patents on biotechnology innovations. BIO publishes several reports, including *Biotechnology Solutions for Everyday Life, New Biotech Tools for a Cleaner Environment*, and the annual *Guide to Biotechnology*.

Center for Bioethics and Human Dignity

2065 Half Day Rd.

Bannockburn, IL 60015

phone: (847) 317-8180 • fax: (847) 317-8101

e-mail: info@cbhd.org • Web site: http://cbhd.org

The center works to help individuals and organizations address the pressing bioethical challenges of the day, including genetic intervention and reproductive technologies. It opposes cloning, human genetic modification, and embryonic stem cell research. The center publishes many position papers and editorials on its Web site.

Center for Food Safety (CFS)

660 Pennsylvania Ave. SE, Suite 302

Washington, DC 20003

phone: (202) 547-9359 • fax: (202) 547-9429

e-mail: office@centerforfoodsafety.org

Web site: www.centerforfoodsafety.org

CFS is a nonprofit public interest and environmental advocacy membership organization that opposes the genetic engineering of plants and animals. The center works to prevent the approval, commercialization, and release of any new genetically engineered crops until they have been thoroughly tested and found safe in human health and the environment. CFS maintains that any foods that already contain genetically engineered ingredients should be clearly labeled. It publishes a quarterly newsletter, the quarterly journal *Food Safety Review*, and several reports on the dangers of genetically modified food.

Center for Genetics and Society

436 14th St., Suite 700

Oakland, CA 94612

phone: (510) 625-0819 • fax: (510) 625-0874

Web site: www.genetics-and-society.org

The center encourages responsible uses and effective societal governance of new human genetic and reproductive technologies. It supports benign and beneficent medical applications of the new human genetic and reproductive technologies and opposes those applications that objectify and commodify human life and threaten to divide human society. The center publishes a newsletter, and its Web site provides information on government technology policies, media coverage of bioethics issues, and other topics.

Clone Rights United Front/Clone Rights Action Center

506 Hudson St.

New York, NY 10014

phone: (212) 255-1439 • fax: (212) 463-0435

e-mail: r.wicker@verizon.net • Web site: www.clonerights.org

The Clone Rights United Front began as a one-issue reproductive rights organization. It was organized to oppose legislation that would make cloning a human being a felony. It is dedicated to the principle that reproductive rights, including cloning, are guaranteed by the Constitution and that each citizen has the right to decide if, when, and how to reproduce. Its Web site has links to Congressional testimony opposing a ban on human cloning and editorials supporting cloning.

Council for Responsible Genetics (CRG)

5 Upland Rd., Suite 3

Cambridge, MA 02140

phone: (617) 868-0870 • fax: (617) 491-5344

e-mail: crg@gene-watch.org • Web site: www.gene-watch.org

CRG works to foster public debate about the social, ethical, and environmental implications of genetic technologies. The council works through the media and concerned citizens to distribute accurate information and represent the public interest on emerging issues in biotechnology. Among its publications is *GeneWatch*, a bimonthly magazine that first began advocating for a Genetic Bill of Rights in 2000.

National Institutes of Health (NIH)

9000 Rockville Pike

Bethesda, MD 20892

phone: (301) 4496-4000

Web site: www.stemcells.nih.gov

The NIH is the federal government's primary agency for the support of biomedical research. It is the government agency responsible for developing guidelines for research on stem cells. Its Web site includes numerous links to articles about stem cell research and frequently asked questions.

Pew Initiative on Food and Biotechnology

1331 H St., Suite 900

Washington, DC 20005

phone: (202) 347-9044 • fax: (202) 347-9047

Web site: www.pewagbiotech.org

The Pew Initiative on Food and Biotechnology strives to be an independent and objective source of credible information on agricultural biotechnology for the public, media, and policy makers. It sponsors conferences and workshops to encourage debate and dialogue on agricultural biotechnology so that consumers and policy makers can make informed decisions. Among its publications are the reports *Options for Future Discussions on Genetically Modified and Cloned Animals* and *Engineering Animals: Ethical Issues and Deliberative Institutions.*

Stem Cell Research Foundation (SCRF)

22512 Gateway Center Dr.

Clarksburg, MD 200871

phone: (877) 842-3442

Web site: www.stemcellresearchfoundation.org

SCRF supports innovative clinical stem cell therapy research. The foundation's goal is to educate the public and conduct fund-raising for stem cell research. It publishes a newsletter, an annual report, and the brochure *Stem Cell Research: A Revolution in Medicine.*

U.S. Conference of Catholic Bishops

3211 4th St. NE

Washington, DC 20017-1194

phone: (202) 541-3000 • fax: (202) 541-3054

e-mail: pro-life@usccb.org • Web site: www.usccb.org

The U.S. Conference of Catholic Bishops advocates a legislative ban and restrictions on abortion. Its publications include the bulletin *Stem Cell Research and Human Cloning* and the brochure *A People of Life.*

For Further Research

Books

Miguel A. Altieri, *Genetic Engineering in Agriculture: The Myths, Environmental Risks, and Alternatives.* 2nd ed. Oakland, CA: Food First, 2004.

John C. Avise, *The Hope, Hype, and Reality of Genetic Engineering: Remarkable Stories from Agriculture, Industry, Medicine, and the Environment.* New York: Oxford University Press, 2004.

Elaine Dewar, *The Second Tree: Stem Cells, Clones, Chimeras, and Quests for Immortality.* New York: Carroll and Graf, 2004.

Karl Drlica, *Understanding DNA and Gene Cloning.* 4th ed. Hoboken, NJ: Wiley, 2004.

Nina Federoff and Nancy Marie Brown, *Mendel in the Kitchen: A Scientist's View of Genetically Modified Foods.* Washington, DC: Joseph Henry, 2004.

Jonathan Glover, *Choosing Children: Genes, Disability, and Design.* New York: Oxford University Press, 2006.

Eric S. Grace, *Biotechnology Unzipped: Promises and Realities.* Rev. 2nd ed. Washington, DC: Joseph Henry, 2006.

Arlene Judith Klotzko, *A Clone of Your Own? The Science and Ethics of Cloning.* New York: Cambridge University Press, 2006.

G.H. Liang and D.Z. Skinner, *Genetically Modified Crops: Their Development, Uses, and Risks.* New York: Food Products, 2004.

Gary Marcus, *The Birth of the Mind: How a Tiny Number of Genes Creates the Complexities of Human Thought.* New York: Basic Books, 2004.

Bill McKibben, *Enough: Staying Human in an Engineered Age.* New York: Times, 2003.

Ramez Naam, *More than Human: Embracing the Promise of Biological Enhancement.* New York: Broadway, 2005.

Matt Ridley, *Nature via Nurture: Genes, Experience, and What Makes Us Human.* New York: HarperCollins, 2003.

Christopher Thomas Scott, *Stem Cell Now: From the Experiment That Shook the World to the New Politics of Life.* New York: Pi, 2006.

Pete Shanks, *Human Genetic Engineering: A Guide for Activists, Skeptics, and the Very Perplexed.* New York: Nation, 2005.

Jennifer A. Thomson, *Seeds for the Future: The Impact of Genetically Modified Crops on the Environment.* Ithaca, NY: Cornell University Press, 2007.

James D. Watson with Andrew Berry, *DNA: The Secret of Life.* New York: Knopf, 2003.

Jonathan Weiner, *His Brother's Keeper: A Story from the Edge of Medicine.* New York: Ecco, 2004.

Periodicals

Clifton E. Anderson, "Biotech on the Farm: Realizing the Promise," *Futurist*, September/October 2005.

Stephen L. Baird, "Designer Babies: Eugenics Repackaged or Consumer Options?" *Technology Teacher*, April 2007.

John Bryant, "Birds, Bees, and Superweeds," *Biological Sciences Review*, November 2004.

Arthur L. Caplan, "Does Stem Cell Advance Provide an Ethical Out?" *MSNBC.com*, June 6, 2007.

Denise Caruso, "A Challenge to Gene Theory, a Tougher Look at Biotech," *New York Times*, July 1, 2007.

Eric Cohen, "Stem-Cell Sense," *National Review Online*, May 25, 2006.

Marc Gunther, "Attack of the Mutant Rice," *Fortune*, July 9, 2007.

Horace Freeland Judson, "The Glimmering Promise of Gene Therapy," *Technology Review*, November/December 2006.

Fraser Los, "The Terminator," *Alternatives Journal*, August 2006.

Stefan Lovgren, "One-Fifth of Human Genes Have Been Patented, Study Reveals," *National Geographic News*, October 13, 2005.

Thomas H. Maugh II, "Fertility Procedure Actually Cuts Birth Rate, Study Finds," *Los Angeles Times*, July 5, 2007.

Jorge E. Mayer, "The Golden Rice Controversy: Useless Science or Unfounded Criticism?" *BioScience*, September 2005.

Jonathan Moreno and Sam Berger, "Stem-Cell Back and Forth," *National Review*, June 3, 2006.

New York Times, "Safe as Milk?" January 6, 2007.

John W. Radin, "How Safe Are Genetically Engineered Crops?" *Agricultural Research*, September 2004.

Wade Roush, "Genetic Savings and Clone: No Pet Project: Can It Cash In on Cloned Cats?" *Technology Review*, March 2005.

William Saletan, "The Organ Factory," *Slate*, July 29, 2005.

Michael J. Sandel, "The Case Against Perfection," *Atlantic Monthly*, April 2004.

Stephanie Simon, "Stem Cell Dissent Roils States," *Los Angeles Times*, August 1, 2007.

Wesley J. Smith, "The Great Stem Cell Coverup," *Weekly Standard*, August 7, 2006.

David Suzuki, "A Little Knowledge," *New Scientist*, September 23, 2006.

Eric G. Swedin, "Designing Babies: A Eugenics Race with China?" *Futurist*, May/June 2006.

H. Lee Sweeney, "Gene Doping," *Scientific American*, June 21, 2004.

Joshua Tomkins, "Can a Virus Kill Cancer?" *Popular Science*, May 1, 2005.

Lisa Turner, "Playing with Our Food," *Better Nutrition*, April 2007.

Carl Zimmer, "How to Program a Cat," *Newsweek*, October 25, 2004.

Web Sites

Americans to Ban Cloning (ABC) (www.cloninginformation.org).

Campaign to Label Genetically Engineered Foods (www.thecampaign .org).

Center for Consumer Freedom (www.consumerfreedom.com).

Clonaid (www.clonaid.com).

Coalition for the Advancement of Medical Research (CAMR) (www. camradvocacy.org).

Food and Drug Administration (www.fda.gov).

Human Cloning Foundation (www.humancloning.org).

Organic Consumers Association (www.organicconsumers.org).

The Reproductive Cloning Network (www.reproductivecloning.net).

Source Notes

Overview

1. Chris Seck, "Arguing For and Against Genetic Engineering," *Stanford Review*, June 8, 2007. www.stanfordreview.org.
2. Miguel A. Altieri, *Genetic Engineering in Agriculture: The Myths, Environmental Risks, and Alternatives*. 2nd ed. Oakland, CA: Food First, 2004, p. 33.
3. Osagie K. Obasogie, "Gene Therapy Risky Business for Patients," *Seattle Post-Intelligencer*, August 16, 2007. www.seattlepi.nwsource.com.
4. W. French Anderson, "The Best of Times, the Worst of Times," *Science*, April 28, 2000, p. 629.
5. Quoted in Bill McKibben, *Enough: Staying Human in an Engineered Age*. New York: Times, 2003, pp. 183–84.
6. Marcy Darnovsky, "Human Germline Manipulation and Cloning as Women's Issues," *GeneWatch*, July 2001. www.gene-watch.org.
7. Josh Mankiewicsz with Ron Reagan, "Ron Reagan Defends Stem Cell Research," *Dateline*, July 28, 2004. www.MSNBC.com.
8. David Christensen, "Patients, Not Politics," *National Review Online*, June 7, 2007. www.nationalreview.com.
9. McKibben, *Enough*, p. 128.
10. Arlene Judith Klotzko, *A Clone of Your Own? The Science and Ethics of Cloning*. New York: Cambridge University Press, 2006, p. 151.
11. Quoted in Kristen Philipkoski, "Canada Closes Door on Cloning," *Wired*, March 17, 2004. www.wired.com.

Is Genetic Engineering Safe in Food and Agriculture?

12. Quoted in *Pro Farmer*, "Monsanto Guarantees Roundup Ready System Will Improve Soybean Profits," July 31, 2000. www.biotech-info.net.
13. Quoted in C. Neal Stewart Jr., *Genetically Modified Planet: Environmental Impacts of Genetically Engineered Plants*. New York: Oxford University Press, 2004, p. 3.
14. Kristina Hubbard, *A Guide to Genetically Modified Alfalfa*. Billings, MT: Western Organization of Resource Councils, 2006, p. 17. www.worc.org.
15. Graham Brookes and Peter Barfoot, "GM Crops: The Global Economic and Environmental Impact—the First Nine Years, 1996–2004," *AgBioForum*, 2005, p. 193.
16. Jeffrey M. Smith, "Plant-Incorporated Protectants; Potential Revisions to Current Production Regulations," testimony before the Environmental Protection Agency, May 22, 2007.
17. Quoted in Smith, "Plant-Incorporated Protectants."
18. Quoted in Brad Stone, Food and Drug Administration Press Release, May 18, 1994. www.fda.gov.
19. Golden Rice Humanitarian Board, "Vitamin A Deficiency-Related Disorders (VADD): The Importance of Micronutrients," 2006. www.goldenrice.org.
20. Altieri, *Genetic Engineering in Agriculture*, p. 33.

Is Genetic Engineering Safe in Humans?

21. Anuja Dokras, "Pre-Implantation Genetic Diagnosis," *Hygeia*. www.hygeia.org.
22. Quoted in *BBC News*, "Watchdog Backs More Embryo Checks," May 10, 2006.
23. Quoted in *BBC News*, "Watchdog Backs More Embryo Checks."
24. Samuel Hensley, "Designer Babies: One Step Closer," July 1, 2004. www.cbhd.org.

25. Quoted in Andy Coghlan, "Gene Therapy Success for Parkinson's Patients," *NewScientist.com*, June 22, 2007.

26. Ramez Naam, *More than Human: Embracing the Promise of Biological Enhancement.* New York: Broadway, 2005, p. 5.

27. Quoted in Australian Society for Medical Research, "Expert Says Genetic Technology Could Enhance Our Children's Well-Being," June 8, 2005. www.asmr.org.au.

28. Quoted in Wendy Carlisle, "Back-Door Eugenics," *Encounter*, ABC Radio National, November 18, 2001. www.abc.net.au.

29. Quoted in John Sutherland, "The Ideas Interview: Julian Savulescu," *Guardian*, October 10, 2005. www.guardian.co.uk.

30. Marilyn E. Coors, "Genetic Enhancement: Custom Kids and Chimeras," U.S. Conference of Catholic Bishops. www.usccb.org.

Is Human Cloning Ethical?

31. President's Council on Bioethics, *Human Cloning and Human Dignity.* Washington, DC: President's Council on Bioethics, 2002, p. xxvii.

32. President's Council on Bioethics, *Human Cloning and Human Dignity*, p. xxviii.

33. Julian Savulescu, "Equality, Cloning, and Clonism: Why We Must Clone," Reproductive Cloning Network. www.reproductivecloning.net.

34. Wesley J. Smith, "The Great Stem Cell Coverup," *Weekly Standard*, August 7, 2006. www.weeklystandard.com.

35. Wesley J. Smith, "The False Promise of Therapeutic Cloning," *National Right to Life News*, October 16, 2003.

36. Christopher Reeve, testimony before the U.S. Senate Committee on Health, Education, Labor, and Pension, March 5, 2002.

37. Charles Krauthammer, "Statement of Dr. Krauthammer," in President's Council on Bioethics, *Human Cloning and Human Dignity: An Ethical Inquiry.* Washington, DC: President's Council on Bioethics, 2002, p. 279.

38. Alfred Cioffi, "Human Cloning: Reproductive or Therapeutic?" Catholic Diocese of Charleston. www.catholic-doc.org.

What Policies Should Govern Genetic Engineering?

39. United States Patent and Trademark Office, "General Information Concerning Patents," January 2005. www.uspto.gov.

40. Quoted in Rural Advancement Foundation International, "New Patent Aims to Prevent Farmers from Saving Seed," RAFI Press Release, March 13, 1998. www.biotech-info.net.

41. Quoted in Daniel J. Kevles, "Patenting Life: A Historical Overview of Law, Interests, and Ethics," www.sba.oakland.edu. December 20, 2001.

42. Dan Eramian, "Patents Save Lives," speech to the Global Public Policy Institute and Ecole de Science Politique, Biotechnology Industry Organization, June 24, 2004. www.bio.org.

43. Quoted in Eric S. Grace, *Biotechnology Unzipped: Promises and Realities.* Rev. 2nd ed. Washington, DC: Joseph Henry, 2006, p. 201.

44. Quoted in Associated Press, "U.S. Patent on Tribesman's Blood Raises Ethical Questions," April 20, 1996.

45. Bill Clinton, "Remarks by the President on Cloning," William J. Clinton Foundation, March 4, 1997. www.clintonfoundation.org.

46. George W. Bush, "President Discusses Stem Cell Research," White House, August 9, 2001. www.whitehouse.gov.

47. Quoted in Pete Shanks, *Human Genetic Engineering: A Guide for Activists, Skeptics, and the Very Perplexed.* New York: Nation, 2005, p. 285.

List of Illustrations

Index

About the Author

Tamara L. Roleff is a freelance writer who lives in Southern California with her husband and three golden retrievers.